Teacher's Pack

1

CONTEMPORARY TOPICS

Academic Listening and Note-Taking Skills

THIRD EDITION

Helen Solórzano
Laurie Frazier

Michael Rost
SERIES EDITOR

PEARSON
Longman

Contemporary Topics 1: Intermediate
Academic Listening and Note-Taking Skills
Third Edition

Pearson Education, 10 Bank Street, White Plains, NY 10606

Staff credits: The people who made up the *Contemporary Topics 1* team, representing editorial, production, design, and manufacturing, are Rhea Banker, Danielle Belfiore, Dave Dickey, Christine Edmonds, Nancy Flaggman, Dana Klinek, Amy McCormick, Linda Moser, Carlos Rountree, Jennifer Stem, Leigh Stolle, Paula Van Ells, Kenneth Volcjak, and Pat Wosczyk.
Cover design: Ann France
Text composition: ElectraGraphics, Inc.
Text font: 11/13 Times

ISBN-10: 0-13-242428-2
ISBN-13: 978-0-13-242428-8

PEARSON LONGMAN ON THE WEB

Pearsonlongman.com offers online resources for teachers and students. Access our Companion Websites, our online catalog, and our local offices around the world.

Visit us at **www.pearsonlongman.com**.

Printed in the United States of America

CONTENTS

INTRODUCTION

The *Contemporary Topics* series provides a stimulating, content-based approach that helps students develop their listening, note-taking, and discussion skills while studying relevant topics. Each unit centers around a short academic lecture, with topics drawn from a range of disciplines.

The lectures feature engaging instructors with live student audiences, and take place in authentic lecture hall settings. The multimodal design of each lecture allows for various learning formats for DVD users, including audio- or video-only presentations, optional subtitling, Presentation Points slide support, and pop-up Coaching Tips.

In order to maximize the benefits of content-based instruction, the *Contemporary Topics* series has developed a carefully sequenced eight-step learning methodology. This introduction provides an overview of each of these steps.

Step 1: Connect to the Topic   *Estimated Time: 10 minutes*   This opening section invites students to activate what they already know about the unit topic by connecting it to their own experiences and beliefs. Typically, students fill out a short survey and compare answers with a partner. The teacher acts as a facilitator, having students share ideas about the topic before they explore it further.

Basic Procedure:

- Set the tone for the unit by talking about the image(s) on the page or related current news events.

- Read the introductory paragraph aloud, paraphrasing as necessary.

- Have students complete the survey/activity.

- Ask students to compare answers with a partner, or discuss answers casually as a class.

Methodology Focus: The actual content of students' responses in this initial activity is not as important as their attempt to understand and interact. It is important that all students participate in activating their ideas about the theme of the unit. This engagement helps set the tone of "active listening" throughout the unit. Having students compare answers with a partner helps ensure that every student is on task and thinking about the unit topic.

 ## Step 2: Build Your Vocabulary   *Estimated Time: 15 minutes*   This section familiarizes students with the key content words and phrases from the lecture. Each lecture contains 10–15 key words from the Academic Word List to ensure that students learn core vocabulary needed for academic success. Students read and *listen to* target words in context so that they can better prepare for the upcoming lecture. Students then complete exercises to get an initial understanding of the target lexis of the unit. Interact with Vocabulary! is a supplementary activity that focuses on the syntax and collocations of new vocabulary in the unit.

Basic Procedure:

- Have students listen to the sentences or paragraphs.

- Have students guess the meaning of each boldfaced word and choose the best definition.

- If time permits, try the Interact with Vocabulary! activity to enable students to focus on form as they learn new words and collocations.

Methodology Focus: Vocabulary knowledge and the ability to recognize vocabulary as it is spoken are key predictors of listening comprehension. As such, spending some pre-listening time on recognizing key vocabulary from the lecture will usually increase students' comprehension of the ideas in the lecture. It's best to spend 10–15 minutes on vocabulary preparation. More than this may give students the impression that vocabulary learning is overly important. Research shows that multiple exposures to new words in context is necessary for vocabulary acquisition, so it's not essential that students "master" the vocabulary in this section. Frequent reviews of the vocabulary sections will aid in acquisition.

 Step 3: Focus Your Attention *Estimated Time: 10 minutes* In this section, students learn strategies for listening actively and taking clear notes. Because a major part of "active listening" involves a readiness to deal with comprehension difficulties, this section provides specific tips to help students direct their attention and gain more control of how they listen. The Try It Out! section, based on a short audio extract, allows students to work on listening and note-taking strategies before they get to the main lecture. Typically, examples of actual notes are provided to give students concrete "starter models."

Basic Procedure:

- Go through this section carefully, reading explanations aloud. Draw attention to examples.

- Play the audio for Try It Out! in order to have students experience the given technique.

- After you play the audio extract once or twice, have students compare answers and/or notes with a partner.

Methodology Focus: Active listening involves a number of component strategies for focusing students' attention: predicting, guessing (i.e. using available knowledge to make good guesses), filling in gaps and making connections, monitoring areas where they don't understand, asking questions, and responding personally. Above all, active listening involves curiosity and a desire to understand more deeply. This section provides tips for focusing students' attention that, when learned incrementally, will help them become more active listeners. It is important that students find a specific way to control their attention and concentration as they listen.

 Step 4: Listen to the Lecture *Estimated Time: 20–30 minutes* As the central section of each unit, Listen to the Lecture allows for two full listening cycles: one to focus on "top-down listening" strategies (Listen for Main Ideas) and one to focus on "bottom-up listening" strategies (Listen for Details). In keeping with the principles of content-based instruction, students are provided with several layers of support. In the Before You Listen section, students are guided to activate concepts and vocabulary they already know or studied earlier in the unit.

The lecture can be viewed in video mode or just listened to in audio mode. In video mode, the lecture can be accompanied by the speaker's Presentation Points or by subtitles for reinforcing comprehension (recommended as a final review). Coaching Tips on strategies for listening, note-taking, and critical thinking can also be turned on.

Basic Procedure:

Before You Listen

- Have students go through this section explicitly—for instance, actually writing down a "prediction" when asked.

Listen for Main Ideas

- Have students *close their books* and take notes as they listen.
- Play the lecture through or pause at times. If pausing, it's best to do so at episode boundaries (see Audioscripts in this Teacher's Pack), as these are natural pausing points.
- Have students complete the exercise, working alone, using their notes.
- Check answers, or play the lecture again so students can confirm their answers. If repeating the lecture, have students confirm and expand their notes with books closed.

Listen for Details

- Play the lecture one more time, again with students confirming and expanding their notes. Then have students complete the Listen for Details exercise.

Methodology Focus: The lecture itself is the focal point of each unit, and therefore the focal point of the content-based approach. In this approach, students of course learn grammar, vocabulary, and pronunciation, but always within the context of relevant content, which may make it more memorable. We recommend that you focus on helping students understand the content of each lecture as deeply as possible, and work on specific language skills during the Talk about the Topic, Review Your Notes, and Extend the Topic sections. To better understand the lecture, students can work on two kinds of exercises: "Top-down listening" generally refers to "getting the gist" of what is said, not focusing on all of the details. "Bottom-up listening" generally refers to hearing "the signal"—that is, the exact words, intonations, and syntax that a speaker uses. Effective listening involves both kinds of processing. As teachers, we may naturally assume that "top-down" processing is more important, but research shows that skills in bottom-up processing is *a key determiner of progress* in L2 listening.

 Step 5: Talk about the Topic *Estimated Time: 15 min* Here students gain valuable discussion skills as they talk about the lecture. Discussion skills are an important part of academic success, and most students benefit from structured practice. In these activities, students listen to a short "model discussion" involving both native and non-native speakers, and identify the speaking strategies and gambits that are used. They then attempt to use some of those strategies in their own discussion groups.

Basic Procedure:

- Have students close their books and listen to the discussion.
- With books open, students may listen again and complete Parts A and B to show a basic understanding of the discussion. Alternatively, you can have students answer general comprehension questions: What was this discussion about? What happened in this discussion? etc.

- Next, have students work in groups of three to five, ideally. They should choose a topic and discuss. They should try to use the discussion strategies they have learned in this or previous units.

Methodology Focus: The first two activities in this section are awareness-raising: We want students to understand the content of the discussion *and* try to identify the types of "discourse strategies" that the study group students are using to make the discussion go well. Discussion ability involves a combination of verbal and nonverbal skills. If showing the video, encourage students to focus on the nonverbal actions of the student speakers: their body language (posture), gaze (direction of eyes on other speakers), and back-channeling (signals to show they are paying attention). Speaking strategies develop incrementally. It's important to have students try out different types of strategies in order to see how they may or may not help students express themselves more fully.

Step 6: Review Your Notes *Estimated Time: 15 minutes* Using notes for review and discussion is an important study skill that is developed in this section. Students are guided in reviewing the content of the unit, clarifying concepts, and preparing for the Unit Test. Incomplete, abbreviated examples of actual notes are provided to help students not only review for the test but also compare and improve their own note-taking skills.

Basic Procedure:

- Have students take out their notes and, with a partner, *take turns* explaining the ideas from the lecture.

- Then have them complete the partial notes.

- Ask if there are any questions about the lecture or anything in their notes. You may wish to preview the Unit Test to be sure that students have discussed the items that will be on it.

Methodology Focus: This section "completes the loop" on note-taking. Research shows that the value of note-taking for memory building is realized primarily when note-takers review their notes and attempt to reconstruct the content. By making explicit statements about the content of the lecture, students are "pushing" their output. They need to use precise grammar and vocabulary in order to articulate their ideas.

 ## Step 7: Take the Unit Test *Estimated Time: 15 minutes* This activity completes the study cycle of the unit: preparation, listening to the lecture, review of content, and assessment. The Unit Test, contained only in this Teacher's Pack, is to be photocopied and distributed by the teacher. Students complete it in class as they listen to the test questions on the audio CD. The *Contemporary Topics* tests are challenging—intended to motivate students to learn the material thoroughly. The format features an answer sheet with choices; the question "stem" is provided on audio only. Test-taking skills include verbatim recall, paraphrasing, inferencing, and synthesizing information from parts of the lecture.

Basic Procedure:

- Optional: Play the lecture once again.

- Pass out a copy of the Unit Test to each student and go over the directions.

- Play the audio for the test one time as students complete the test by circling their answers. You may pause the audio between questions.

- Collect the tests to correct yourself, or have students exchange papers and go over the answers in class. Replay the audio as you go over the correct answers.

Methodology Focus: The tests in *Contemporary Topics* have the question "stem" on audio only—the students can't read it. They have to listen carefully and then choose the correct answer. This format is more challenging than most standardized tests, such as the TOEFL. We chose this challenging format to motivate students to work through the unit diligently and know the content well.

 Step 8: Extend the Topic *Estimated time: 20 minutes* This final section creates a natural extension of the unit topic to areas that are relevant to students. Students first listen to a supplementary media clip drawn from a variety of interesting genres. Typically, students then have a discussion or prepare a class presentation.

Basic Procedure:

- Choose one of the activities, or more if time permits. Review the steps of the activity together.

- Allow time, if possible, for student presentations.

Methodology Focus: An important aspect of a content-based approach is the application, or follow-up step. This step helps students personalize the content of the unit, choosing to develop topics of personal interest. Allowing time for student research and presentations not only increases interest and involvement in the course, but also allows the teacher an opportunity to give individualized feedback that will help students' progress.

By completing these eight steps, students can develop stronger listening, speaking, and note-taking skills and strategies—thereby becoming more confident and independent learners.

Michael Rost
Series Editor

Multimedia Guidelines: With the DVD, you can play the lecture in different modes: video, video with subtitles, video with Coaching Tips, video with Presentation Points, video with Coaching Tips and subtitles, and video with Coaching Tips and Presentation Points. We do not recommend playing the video with both the Presentation Points and subtitles on.

Note that while the DVD is compatible with most computer media players, for optimum viewing we suggest playing the DVD on a television screen (ideally a wide-screen), using a DVD player.

You can also play the lecture as audio only, using the CD.

We recommend that you play the lecture once in "plain" video mode, then once as audio only. For review, you can play the video again with the Presentation Points and/or Coaching Tips turned on. As another review option, students can watch the subtitled version on their own.

Viewing preferences can be selected under SET UP. Or, with a remote control, subtitles can be activated at any time using the caption button, and Presentation Points can be activated at any time using the angle button.

PSYCHOLOGY
Happiness

TEACHING TIPS

UNIT OVERVIEW

In this unit, students will discuss the topic of happiness. The lecture focuses on the field of positive psychology and what research by positive psychologists has revealed about the characteristics of happy people. Follow-up projects allow students to engage in exercises designed by positive psychologists to help people become happier.

Connect to the Topic *page 2*   *~10 minutes*

As a warm-up activity, consider having students guess what the three photos have in common (people who are happy about something). In the introduction, students learn the meaning of *positive psychology*. Then they take a survey about their beliefs about happiness. Students rank what they consider most important for happiness, then compare their rankings with other students.

Build Your Vocabulary *pages 3–4*   *~15 minutes*

Students study the following words and phrases related to psychology and happiness:

achieve	find out	method
attitude about	goal	personality
characteristics	goal of	relevant
connection	gratitude	requirement
connection to	gratitude toward	requirement for
data	income	research
data on	income from	research on
depend on	level of	strengths
developed by	measure	

For the Interact with Vocabulary! activity, you may want to encourage students to first notice the boldfaced words and explain that the boldfaced words form collocations when paired correctly.

Focus Your Attention *page 5*   *~10 minutes*

Students learn cues that lecturers use at the beginning of a lecture to indicate the lecture topic and organization:

Today . . .	*I'd like to . . .*	*get started with . . .*
In today's lecture . . .	*I want to . . .*	*start with . . .*
First . . .	*I'm/We're going to . . .*	*talk about . . .*
Then . . .	*We'll . . .*	*look at . . .*
After that, . . .		
Finally, . . .		

Listen to the Lecture *pages 6–7*   ~30 minutes

Students consider statements about happiness (Before You Listen) before listening to the unit lecture on happiness. They then check main ideas mentioned in the lecture (Listen for Main Ideas) and answer true/false questions about the details (Listen for Details).
Lecture video time: 7 min. 14 sec.   *Number of episodes: 9*

NOTE

Remember that with the DVD, you can play the lecture in different modes: video, video with Presentation Points, video with Coaching Tips, video with subtitles, video with subtitles and Coaching Tips, and video with Coaching Tips and Presentation Points. We recommend that you play the lecture once in "plain" video mode, then once as audio only. For review, you can play the video again with the Presentation Points and/or Coaching Tips turned on. As another review option, students can watch the subtitled version on their own.

Talk about the Topic *page 8*   ~20 minutes

Four students—Mia, Manny, Hannah, and River—discuss the lecture. Part A focuses on matching these students with comments or ideas from the discussion. In Part B, your students work on these discussion strategies:

- Agreeing: "Yeah, I know what you mean."
- Disagreeing: "Really? I don't think so."

For Part C, students are encouraged to use the discussion strategies they've learned. They may use phrases from the student discussion and/or the Discussion Strategy box, or they may come up with their own.
Student discussion video time: 1 min. 6 sec.

Review Your Notes *page 9*   ~15 minutes

Students focus on reconstructing their notes, paying attention to key words and main ideas.

BONUS ACTIVITY

You can supplement this activity by having students use their notes to summarize parts of the lecture with a partner.

Take the Unit Test *Teacher's Pack page 7*   ~15 minutes

You may want to play the lecture again just before giving the test. Students answer standard test questions about the content of the lecture. Specifically, the test covers the following: how psychologists measure happiness, the characteristics of happy people, and exercises that people can do to feel happier.

Extend the Topic *pages 10–11*   ~30 minutes

- Listening and Discussion: Students listen to and discuss an interview between a psychology researcher and someone who has tried a happiness exercise.
- Project/Presentation: Students complete a survey to determine their own strengths, complete a happiness exercise, and report their results to the class.

Focus Your Attention:
Try It Out! *page 5*

Speaker: Good afternoon, everybody. Today, we're going to talk about positive psychology. First, I want to start with a definition of positive psychology. After that, we'll look at the goals of positive psychology—what positive psychologists are trying to learn. Finally, we're going to discuss some research done by positive psychologists . . . So, is everyone clear on the topic? . . .

Listen for Main Ideas and Listen for Details *pages 6–7*

Psychology lecturer: **E1** Good morning everybody. Today I want to get started with the main topic of this course: happiness. First I want to talk about how psychologists like myself measure happiness. Then we'll look at some common characteristics of happy people. And finally, we'll look at whether or not we can change our level of happiness—in other words, whether we can learn to be happier. **E2** OK, so we all know what it's like to feel happy, right? But how do we measure happiness? One common method psychologists use is interviewing people. First, we ask them questions to find out how happy they are— how happy they feel in general. Then we gather information about them—like their age, health, income, and so on. We use all of this data to determine the most common characteristics of happy people. **E3** So what have psychologists learned? Well, there are a few characteristics we know are not relevant to happiness. One of them is having a lot of money. As long as people have enough money for a home, food, and clothing, having more money doesn't make people happier. So, money doesn't buy happiness. Are you surprised? Another thing that is not connected to happiness is having more education. People with a lot of education are no happier than people with little education. So now maybe you're questioning your decision to take this class, huh? Finally, a third characteristic that is not a requirement for happiness is youth—being young. In fact, the opposite is true. One study found that sixty- to sixty-four-year-olds are actually happier than twenty- to twenty-four-year-olds. **E4** So we know that money, education, and youth are not important to happiness. Then what is? Well, there's no one way to achieve happiness. But there are a few specific characteristics that happy people have in common. One very important characteristic is family and friends. A study of students at the University of Illinois found that the happiest students had strong connections to family and friends, and that they made time to spend with them. Another common feature of happy people is that they have religious beliefs or a belief in something bigger than themselves. This helps them feel that life has significance, or meaning. A third important thing about happy people is that they set goals for themselves. In the workplace or in their personal lives, they establish goals around things they find interesting or things that allow them to use their strengths. **E5** Now, another question psychologists have tried to resolve is, can we change how happy we are? Can we learn to be happier? Some psychologists think the answer is "No, we can't." This is because research shows that happiness depends a lot on our personality—the kind of person we are. Some people just have more positive attitudes about life than others. We've all noticed this, right? And because it's difficult for people to change their personalities, some psychologists think that we stay at about the same level of happiness throughout our lives. **E6** But many of us in the field of positive psychology believe we can change—that we can consciously learn to be happier. Positive psychologists have developed some exercises that people can do to feel happier. One of these is called the "Gratitude Visit." In this exercise, people write a letter to someone they want to thank. For example: a parent, a friend, a teacher—someone they feel has helped them in their life. But they don't send the letter. Instead, they visit the person and read the letter to them. **E7** Now, research shows this really works to make the person who wrote the letter feel happier. Why? First, it helps them feel more connected to others. And remember, that is very important for happiness. Second, the people are giving something—in this case, their thanks—to someone else. And giving or helping others makes us feel better about ourselves. It helps us feel that our lives have meaning. **E8** In addition to the Gratitude Visit, psychologists have developed other exercises that help people focus on the positive things in their lives, and help them use their strengths to achieve goals. And studies have shown that these exercises can help people feel better. However, they do have limits. For one thing, each exercise only works for a certain amount of time. For example, the Gratitude Visit only makes people happier for about three months. And, of course, we can't become a lot happier. Remember, we can't totally change our personalities. You can't take a really unhappy, negative person and make him or her feel super-happy all the time. **E9** But, I do believe that if we really want to, we can all learn ways to feel better, to feel the best that we can. And you're going to find this out for yourselves. For the next time, I'd like you to look into choosing your own happiness exercise.

Coaching Tips

[1] **Note-taking: Organizing main ideas** Were you listening for the main ideas of the lecture? The first is how happiness is measured. What's the second? What's the third? If you didn't hear them, listen again. This will tell you the ideas that the lecturer is about to present, and help you organize your notes. So far, your notes might look like this: [see video for note-taking example].

[2] **Critical Thinking: Predicting** *Predicting* means making an informed guess about what you expect to hear next. Predicting what is coming up next in a lecture can help you stay focused. What do you predict the lecturer will speak about next? Hint: Did you write down a topic for main idea number three?

[3] **Critical Thinking: Identifying point of view** What does the lecturer believe? Does she agree with psychologists who say we can't change our level of happiness? Or does she disagree? By using the word *us*, the lecturer makes it clear that she works in the field of positive psychology. And we know that positive psychologists believe people can change.

[4] **Critical Thinking: Guessing** Think about what limits happiness exercises might have. Try to list one or two possibilities. Guessing is a good way to explore new ideas. You don't have to be right! Now listen to the lecturer talk about some limits. Are they similar to the limits you thought of?

Talk about the Topic *page 8*

Mia: I think this class is going to be really fun! I mean, we're studying happiness!

Hannah: Yeah, I know what you mean. This is a cool topic.

Mia: Maybe the ideas from this course can completely change people's lives! Like, maybe I'll become happier!

River: Really? I don't think so. I don't think these ideas can really work. I mean, we're either happy people or we're not, like she said.

Manny: Yeah, exactly. Like, did you guys get the "Gratitude Visit"? I mean, is that really going to make you happier for . . . How long did she say?

Hannah: Three months.

Manny: I doubt it. Maybe like a week. But then you're yourself again.

Mia: I'm sorry. I don't agree. I think a really positive experience can stay with you a long time. Like I said, it can change your life!

River: But don't forget: Not all psychologists believe you can learn to be happier—do you have that in your notes?

Mia: Yeah, I guess so. I guess I'm just a positive thinker.

Take the Unit Test

1. How do psychologists measure happiness?
2. What have psychologists learned about happiness?
3. Which of the three characteristics are connected to happiness?
4. Which of the following is *not* a characteristic of happy people?
5. Listen to part of the lecture again: *Now, another question psychologists have tried to resolve is, can we change how happy we are? Can we learn to be happier? Some psychologists think the answer is "No, we can't."* Why does the speaker say, "Some psychologists think the answer is 'No, we can't.'"?
6. How can people learn to feel happier?
7. How do you thank someone during the Gratitude Visit?
8. Why does a Gratitude Visit make people feel happier?
9. What do psychologists say about our personalities?
10. What is one of the main points of the lecture?

Extend the Topic *page 10*

Clerk: . . . And, so I work at a grocery store. I've been there about three years now. Anyway, in the beginning, my job felt really boring . . .

Researcher: Uh-huh.

Clerk: The first year or so, I hated my job. I hated going to work. Then I tried this happiness exercise called "Using Your Strengths."

Researcher: Ah. Tell me about that.

Clerk: Well, first, I had to think about my strengths—you know, my strong points. One of my strengths is getting along with people. I like meeting people, and I make friends easily. So, for the exercise, I had to think of ways to use my strength every day. So I set a goal to have more conversations—even small conversations—every day with people at work. And after just one day, I felt happier. I felt more connected with people. Now, I really enjoy my work.

Researcher: Hmm. Interesting . . .

Build Your Vocabulary *pages 3–4*

A. 1. c 2. b 3. a 4. c 5. d 6. a 7. b 8. c 9. a 10. b 11. d 12. a 13. c 14. b **B. Interact with Vocabulary!** 1. about 2. to 3. on 4. on 5. by 6. out 7. of 8. toward 9. from 10. of 11. for 12. on

Focus Your Attention *page 5*

A. Today <u>positive</u> psychology; 1) <u>definition</u>; 2) <u>goals</u>; 3) <u>research</u>

Listen for Main Ideas *page 6*

B. Check: 1, 5, 7

Listen for Details *page 7*

B. 1. T 2. F (higher level) 3. T 4. F (goals that are interesting or that use their strengths) 5. F (cannot easily change) 6. T 7. F (write then read a letter to someone they want to thank) 8. T 9. F (feel better/not a lot happier)

Talk about the Topic *page 8*

A. *Suggested answers:* 1. Mia, Hannah (Note: You may want to explain that Mia's use of the word "fun" to describe the class also implies that she finds it "interesting.") 2. Mia 3. Manny, River **B.** Agreeing: 1, 3, 6; Disagreeing: 2, 4, 5

Review Your Notes *page 9*

Measuring happiness: Interview people about how they feel and collect data; Unimportant characteristics: education, money, youth; Important characteristics: friends/family, beliefs, goals; Learn to be happier: exercises like the Gratitude Visit

Take the Unit Test

1. c 2. b 3. b 4. b 5. a 6. a 7. b 8. a 9. a 10. a

Extend the Topic *page 10*

A. 1. He thinks about his strengths. Then he sets a goal related to one of his strengths. Then he acts on it. 2. He feels more connected to people. 3. It's ongoing. You use your strengths.

PSYCHOLOGY: Happiness

 Listen to each question. Circle the letter of the correct answer.

1. a. They watch people in daily life.
   b. They give people a happiness test.
   c. They interview people about their lives.
   d. They make Gratitude Visits.

2. a. Most people say they are happy.
   b. Happy people share some common characteristics.
   c. People are happy for different reasons.
   d. Happiness is difficult to measure.

3. a. intelligence, goals, and experience
   b. family and friends, religion/beliefs, and goals
   c. money, education, and youth
   d. education, work, and friends

4. a. having a connection with family and friends
   b. having a lot of money
   c. having religious or other beliefs
   d. having goals

5. a. to introduce a different opinion
   b. to explain her own opinion
   c. to describe what most people think
   d. to ask what the students think

6. a. by doing exercises that focus on the positive things in their lives
   b. by talking to a psychologist about their feelings
   c. by not thinking about their problems
   d. by changing their personalities

7. a. You tell your friends about your visit.
   b. You visit the person and read him or her a letter.
   c. You ask the person to visit you at your house.
   d. You invite the person to visit a special place with you.

8. a. It helps them feel connected to others by thanking them.
   b. It is part of their religious beliefs.
   c. It allows them to set goals for themselves.
   d. It helps them get a better education.

9. a. Our level of happiness depends a lot on our personality.
   b. We can totally change our personalities.
   c. People have different personalities.
   d. Our personalities help us feel connected to others.

10. a. People can do things to become happier.
    b. Unhappy people can totally change their personalities.
    c. Some people are happier than others.
    d. Happiness is studied by psychologists.

LINGUISTICS
A Time to Learn

UNIT OVERVIEW

In this unit, students will discuss the topic of language learning. The lecture focuses on the critical period hypothesis, the ways adults and children learn languages, and the various factors that contribute to language learning. Follow-up projects allow students to learn firsthand about a second language learner's experience.

Connect to the Topic *page 12*   *~10 minutes*

As a warm-up activity, consider having students work in groups to see how many of the messages in the "thank you" graphic they can translate (all are expressions of thanks). In the survey, students work in groups to explore their beliefs about how children and adults learn languages. Then they compare their opinions.

Build Your Vocabulary *pages 13–14*   *~15 minutes*

Students study the following words and phrases related to linguistics and language learning:

acquisition	for a period of	period
brain	time	role
controlled by	ideal	(an important) role
(the) brain	ideal time	in
critical	in an environment	second language
critical time	motivation	acquisition
environment	motivation for	theory
factor	obvious	theories on
factor for	obvious reason for	

For the Interact with Vocabulary! activity, you may want to encourage students to first notice the boldfaced words. Figuring out these collocations can help students more quickly unscramble the sentences.

Focus Your Attention *page 15*   *~10 minutes*

Students learn how lecturers use rhetorical questions to signal new or important information. Students learn to recognize the nonverbal cues (such as pausing and looking at listeners) that lecturers use to signal rhetorical questions.

Listen to the Lecture *pages 16–17*   *~30 minutes*

Students choose what they think is the most important factor for learning a second language (Before You Listen) before listening to the unit lecture on language learning. They answer multiple-choice questions (Listen for Main Ideas) and identify details mentioned in the lecture (Listen for Details).
Lecture video time: 5 min. 21 sec.   *Number of episodes: 8*

NOTE

Remember that with the DVD, you can play the lecture in different modes: video, video with Presentation Points, video with Coaching Tips, video with subtitles, video with subtitles and Coaching Tips, and video with Coaching Tips and Presentation Points. (We do not recommend playing the video with both the Presentation Points and subtitles on.) You can also play the lecture as audio only, using the CD.

Talk about the Topic *page 18*   *~20 minutes*

Four students—Molly, Rob, Alana, and Ayman—discuss the lecture. Part A focuses on matching these students with comments from the discussion. In Part B, your students work on these discussion strategies:

- Asking for opinions or ideas: "OK, so what does everyone think about this 'critical period' theory?"
- Asking for clarification or confirmation: "Really? How so?"

BONUS ACTIVITY

You can supplement this activity by having students compare their opinions with the opinions of the students in the discussion.

For Part C, students are encouraged to use the discussion strategies they've learned. They may use phrases from the student discussion and/or the Discussion Strategy box, or they may come up with their own.
Student discussion video time: 1 min. 20 sec.

Review Your Notes *page 19*   *~15 minutes*

Students focus on reconstructing their notes, paying attention to key words, definitions, and main ideas.

BONUS ACTIVITY

You can supplement this activity by having students use their notes to summarize parts of the lecture with a partner.

Take the Unit Test *Teacher's Pack page 13*   *~15 minutes*

You may want to play the lecture again just before giving the test. Students answer standard test questions about the content of the lecture. Specifically, the test covers the following: factors that affect language learning and the critical period for language learning.

Extend the Topic *pages 20–21*   *~30 minutes*

- Listening and Discussion: Students listen to an ad for a language school in which a businesswoman describes her approach to language learning.
- Project/Presentation: Students interview a successful language learner and share with the class what they learned.

Focus Your Attention:
Try It Out! *page 15*

Speaker: In this class, we're going to look at how people learn language. First, let's talk about babies: How do babies learn language? Well, they learn by hearing language around them. They're ready to learn language at birth. Parents don't have to teach babies how to talk—not like we're taught to read and write in school. No, we just talk to a baby, and the baby will learn. Now you may wonder, why do babies learn so easily? Well that's a very interesting question . . .

Listen for Main Ideas and Listen
for Details *pages 16–17*

Linguistics lecturer: E1 Now, let me ask, how many of you have studied a new language, not the language you grew up speaking? Show of hands? All right, OK. Well, today we're going to look at second language acquisition—that is, learning a second language. And one question that linguists like myself have tried to answer for many years is, why is it considerably easier for kids to learn a second language than adults? Now, we're going to look at a few different theories about this. First we'll look at a theory that says there's a critical period or phase—or ideal time in life—for language learning. And then we'll talk about other factors, such as the learning environment, attitude, and motivation. **E2** Now, from the show of hands, I see that many of you've had your own personal experience with language learning. And I have recently, too—I started studying Mandarin Chinese—*pu-tong-hua*—this last year. And so I've been going to class, you know, listening to language CDs. And I'm learning, but it's tough. It's tough to learn a new language. And then today, I went into my son's class—he's in first grade now—and one of my son's friends, Zhiwei—he goes by Steven now—he just moved here last fall from China. And when he first came into the class, he didn't speak a word of English. I mean, not one word. But now, he's talking away in English, not always perfectly, but very easily, very fluent. And I'm, like, wow! This is so unfair. We've both been studying a new language for the same amount of time, but he's learning it so much more quickly. **E3** This is, in fact, something that linguists are very interested in—understanding this difference between how kids and adults learn a new language. Now one explanation is that there's a critical period for language learning. Now this theory was first introduced in the 1960s by a linguist named Eric Lenneberg. And Lenneberg's theory says that during childhood, language learning is very easy. Basically our brains are just ready for language learning. But later, starting in adolescence and as we get older, our brains change—we lose this childhood ability, and it becomes more difficult to learn language. And that's why adults have trouble learning a new language. **E4** Well, if you're an adult, that's a bit discouraging, right? You can look at my son's friend Steven, who's six years old, and me, who's twenty-nine-plus, and say, well, OK, Steven is still in the critical phase; his brain works perfectly right now for language learning. But you, you're way past the critical phase, and your brain's already changed, so too bad! I'm sorry. But wait a minute! Is this comparison between me and Steven really fair? I mean, there's an age difference, but there are a lot of other differences as well. Can we really say that my lack of progress learning Chinese is only because I've passed the critical phase? No, no, no. Many people, including linguist Robert DeKeyser, would say no, you have to look at other factors. OK. **E5** Now one obvious factor in second language acquisition is environment—the place where the person is learning. So Steven is here in an all-English environment, where he's speaking English all day at school, and all of his friends speak English. Me, on the other hand, I'm just taking a class two hours a week. So, sure, I listen to my Chinese CDs in my car on the way to work, but other than that, I'm not in an environment where I hear a lot of Chinese. And I wonder, what if it were the other way around? What if I went to China, and was in school all day hearing Chinese? And Steven was studying English only two hours a week. Do you think that would change how well we were each learning the language? Yeah, I'm sure it would. So, environment plays a significant role in language acquisition. **E6** Another factor in second language acquisition is a person's attitude about learning the new language. How do you feel about learning? Now when I was watching Steven in the classroom, playing with his friends, it was clear he didn't feel at all embarrassed about his English language abilities. You know, he can't speak perfectly yet, but when he made a mistake, he didn't care, and neither did his friends. They just kept on playing. Me, on the other hand, I find it very difficult to speak Chinese when I'm not sure what I'm saying. I get very nervous and embarrassed. And, as a result, I don't practice speaking as much as I should. So clearly, a person's attitude about learning is very important in acquiring a second language. **E7** Finally, the last factor we'll look at is motivation. OK, why is the person learning the language? Now, Steven is probably very motivated to learn English. All his friends speak it, so he needs to learn it in order to play with them. I, on the other hand, want to learn Chinese, but I don't need to. So we're both motivated to learn, but perhaps my motivation isn't quite as strong. E8 All right, so, what do we understand about second language acquisition? Well, there does seem to be a critical period in childhood when language learning is much easier. But it's important to look at all the factors—and there are several, including environment, attitude, and motivation—which help decide if someone is going to be a successful language learner. As for me? I'm not ready to give up on Chinese just yet!

Coaching Tips

[1] Note-taking: Organizing main ideas At the beginning of a talk—during the introduction—a speaker usually will tell you the main ideas that he or she plans to cover. Here, the speaker introduces the main topic—second language acquisition—and his plan to talk about two different theories. Now you know what to expect from the lecture and how to set up your notes. Here's one idea: [see video for note-taking example]. [2] Critical Thinking: Thinking of examples An example can help you understand the concepts of a topic. Here, the speaker gives two personal examples of language learning. Do these examples help you understand? How? Maybe you know similar examples. You may want to write your own examples in the margin—or to the side—of your notes. [3] Critical Thinking: Identifying rhetorical questions The speaker asks, "Is this comparison between me and Steven really fair?" Then he asks, "Can we really say that my lack of progress learning Chinese is only because I've passed the critical period?" Do you think he expects answers to these questions? No, not really. These are *rhetorical* questions. While some questions need answers, rhetorical questions do not. Rather, they help you think more deeply about the topic.
[4] Critical Thinking: Predicting You've now heard one of the other factors in language acquisition. This is a good place to predict: What other factors do you think the lecturer will say might make a difference in how a person learns a second language? Hint: Did you take detailed notes during his introduction?

Talk about the Topic *page 18*

Rob: OK, so what does everyone think about this "critical period" theory? Like, the big thing is that it's harder to learn a language if you're an adult, right?

Alana: Actually, speaking from my own experience, I'd say the other factors he mentioned are just as important.

Molly: What other factors?

Alana: Well, attitude, environment, and motivation. Those were big for me.

Molly: Hmm.

Rob: Really? How so? Like what was your experience like?

Alana: Oh, OK, well, I came to the United States from Russia as a teenager, and every time I spoke, I got so nervous. I was afraid people would make fun of me.

Molly: Oh, really? I thought kids learned easily.

Alana: Well, I was in high school, so a little older. Anyway, I made some friends, I watched a lot of TV—and now I feel pretty comfortable talking to anyone.

Molly: Good.

Rob: Ayman, what about you? What was it like for you?

Ayman: Oh, well, to me, the critical period explains a lot. My niece, who's four, came over here when I did—two years ago. And she sounds like you guys.

Rob: Really?

Ayman: She talks like a native speaker. And I'm so jealous!

Molly: Oh, you'll get there, you know, it's just a matter of time . . .

Rob: Oh, definitely.

Molly: . . . and practice.

Rob: I mean, for two years you sound good, definitely.

Molly: Yeah.

Ayman: Yeah.

Rob: I wouldn't worry about it.

Take the Unit Test

1. What is the lecture mainly about?
2. Who is Steven?
3. Why does the speaker compare himself to Steven?
4. What is the critical period for language learning?
5. What is Steven's language learning environment?
6. What is the lecturer's attitude about language learning?
7. What is Steven's motivation for language learning?
8. What language learning factor changes as we get older and our brains change?
9. How does the speaker think he can learn Chinese more successfully?
10. Listen to this excerpt from the lecture: *But it's important to look at all the factors—and there are several, including environment, attitude, and motivation—which help decide if someone is going to be a successful language learner. As for me? I'm not ready to give up on Chinese just yet!* What does the speaker mean when he says, "As for me? I'm not ready to give up on Chinese just yet!"

Extend the Topic *page 20*

Businesswoman: I'm a sales representative, and my company does a lot of business in Japan. To get ahead, I want to learn Japanese—at least conversational Japanese. So I'm taking a class two nights a week at the Lotus Language School. Now when I go on sales trips to Japan, I can practice my new language skills. Speaking Japanese isn't *required* for my job, but I think it'll help me move up in my company. It'll help me become a more effective salesperson, too. Besides, I love the Japanese language and culture, and someday would like to live in Japan for a while. That's my dream, anyway. And Lotus Language School is helping me realize it!

ANSWER KEY

Build Your Vocabulary *pages 13–14*

A. 1. a 2. c 3. b 4. b 5. a 6. c 7. b 8. a 9. c 10. c 11. a **B. Interact with Vocabulary!** 1. on second language acquisition 2. controlled by your brain 3. a critical time for learning 4. in an all-English environment 5. an important factor for doing well 6. the ideal time to listen to my Spanish language CDs 7. strong motivation for learning English 8. reason for learning a new language is 9. French for a short period of time. 10. an important role in their children's lives 11. about theories on language learning

Focus Your Attention *page 15*

A. Babies: How do <u>babies learn language</u>? Why do <u>babies learn so easily</u>?

Listen for Main Ideas *pages 16–17*

B. 1. a 2. a 3. b 4. c 5. c

Listen for Details *page 17*

B. 1. Steven, Lecturer 2. Lecturer 3. Steven, Lecturer 4. Steven 5. Steven 6. Lecturer 7. Lecturer 8. Steven

Talk about the Topic *page 18*

A. 1. Rob 2. Alana 3. Molly 4. Ayman **B.** Asking for opinions or ideas: 1, 4; Asking for clarification: 2, 3

Review Your Notes *page 19*

	Def.	Steven	Lecturer
critical period	the time during childhood, up until adolescence, when language learning is easiest	in this period, learning easily	past this period
environment	the place where a person is learning language	all-English	not Chinese
attitude	how a person feels about learning a language	doesn't care	nervous/ embarrassed
motivation	the reason why a person is learning a language	needs to learn	wants to learn

Take the Unit Test

1. d 2. c 3. d 4. a 5. c 6. a 7. d 8. d 9. d 10. a

Extend the Topic *page 20*

A. 1. to get ahead in her job, to live in Japan someday 2. positive, confident 3. English-speaking / the classroom 4. No, she's an adult.

 **TEST** # LINGUISTICS: A Time to Learn

 Listen to each question. Circle the letter of the correct answer.

1. a. how children learn a new language
   b. problems adults have learning a new language
   c. reasons to learn new languages
   d. factors that affect language learning

2. a. a classmate in the speaker's Chinese class
   b. a student in the speaker's linguistics class
   c. a friend of the speaker's son
   d. a coworker of the speaker

3. a. to complain about his problems learning a new language
   b. to describe how he learns a language
   c. to show the best way to learn a language
   d. to explain the different factors in language learning

4. a. a time in childhood when language learning is easy
   b. how you feel about learning a language
   c. the place where you learn a language
   d. the reason you want to learn a language

5. a. He has studied English for a year.
   b. He is only six years old.
   c. He lives and goes to school in an English-speaking country.
   d. He wants to play with English-speaking friends.

6. a. He gets nervous when he's speaking Chinese.
   b. He has a lot of friends that speak Chinese.
   c. He wants to move to China.
   d. He goes to Chinese class once a week.

7. a. His parents want him to learn.
   b. He is learning English quickly.
   c. He is in the critical period for language learning.
   d. He wants to play with his English-speaking friends.

8. a. our attitude about language learning
   b. our language learning environment
   c. our motivation for language learning
   d. our age

9. a. by practicing more
   b. by studying Chinese in China
   c. by having friends who speak only Chinese
   d. all of the above

10. a. "I'm going to continue studying Chinese."
    b. "I'm not a successful language learner."
    c. "I'm not going to study Chinese anymore."
    d. "Chinese is difficult to learn."

UNIT 3
PUBLIC HEALTH
Sleep

TEACHING TIPS

UNIT OVERVIEW

In this unit, students will explore the topic of sleep deprivation and its effects on health. The lecture focuses on the immediate and long-term effects of sleep deprivation. Follow-up projects allow students to research and report on common sleep problems.

Connect to the Topic *page 22*

~10 minutes

As a warm-up activity, consider having students discuss the meaning of the cartoon of the sleeping parents, then discuss how much they themselves value sleep. Below, students complete a survey about their sleep habits and discuss the results.

Build Your Vocabulary *pages 23–24*

~15 minutes

Students study the following words and phrases related to public health and sleep:

aspect	injured in	shift
consequence	lack of sleep	sleep deprivation
function	likely to	stay up
immediate	link	suffer from
immediate effect on	more likely	work in shifts
impact	percent	
injured	realized	

After the Interact with Vocabulary! activity, you may want to have students practice using the boldfaced words with their partners. Knowing collocations can help students expand their vocabularies and increase their fluency.

Focus Your Attention *page 25*

~10 minutes

Students learn how lecturers use signal phrases for the following:

To introduce a new point:	To give an example:	To emphasize a point:
Now . . .	*One example is . . .*	*In fact, . . .*
Let's start with . . .	*For example, . . .*	*It's clear that . . .*
First, . . .	*For instance, . . .*	*Interesting, huh?*
Next, . . .	*This is illustrated . . .*	
In addition . . .	*Let's look at an example . . .*	
Finally, . . .		

Listen to the Lecture *pages 26–27*

~30 minutes

Students consider what happens to them if they don't get enough sleep (Before You Listen). Then they listen to the unit lecture on the health effects of sleep deprivation. They identify the effects mentioned in the lecture and categorize them as immediate or long-term (Listen for Main Ideas). They also answer multiple-choice questions about details from the lecture (Listen to Details).

Lecture video time: 5 min. 54 sec.   Number of episodes: 9

Talk about the Topic *page 28*   *~20 minutes*

Four students—Rob, Alana, Ayman, and Molly—discuss the lecture. Part A focuses on matching these students with comments or ideas from the discussion. In Part B, your students work on these discussion strategies:

- Expressing an opinion: "This is really interesting to me."
- Paraphrasing: "She said seven to nine hours, so eight hours on average."

BONUS ACTIVITY

You can supplement this activity by having students compare their opinions with the opinions of the students in the discussion.

For Part C, students are encouraged to use the discussion strategies they've learned. They may use phrases from the student discussion and/or the Discussion Strategy box, or they may come up with their own.
Student discussion video time: 1 min. 13 sec.

Review Your Notes *page 29*   *~15 minutes*

Students focus on reconstructing their notes, paying attention to key words and phrases, main ideas, definitions, and examples.

BONUS ACTIVITY

You can supplement this activity by having students use their notes to summarize parts of the lecture with a partner.

Take the Unit Test *Teacher's Pack page 19*   *~15 minutes*

You want to play the lecture again just before giving the test. Students answer standard test questions about the content of the lecture. Specifically, the test covers the following: the definition and effects of sleep deprivation.

Extend the Topic *pages 30–31*   *~30 minutes*

- Listening and Discussion: Students listen to a news report about a school policy designed to help students get more sleep. Then they discuss the effectiveness of the strategy.
- Project/Presentation: Students research different sleep problems and report back on them.

Focus Your Attention:
Try It Out! *page 25*

Speaker: First, let's start with the sleep habits of children. Children need much more sleep than adults. For instance, newborn babies—babies just one to three months old—need up to sixteen hours of sleep each day. They need sleep to grow, and for their brains to develop. So it's clear that sleep is very important for young babies. OK, next thing . . .

Listen for Main Ideas and Listen
for Details *pages 26–27*

Public health lecturer: E1 How many of you got enough sleep last night? Huh, not so many. OK. Well, that's what we're going to cover today—the issue of sleep deprivation, not getting enough sleep. Now, you might say, "Sleep deprivation? Why is this a public health problem?" In fact, there are many serious consequences of not getting enough sleep. So we'll first look at the immediate impact—problems that it causes in your daily life. And then we'll look at the long-term effects—problems that grow over many months or years—especially concerning our health. **E2** Let's start with a definition of sleep deprivation. Most adults need seven to nine hours of sleep every night. So, if you get less than seven hours of sleep on most nights, you'll start suffering from sleep deprivation. Lack of sleep has serious effects on the brain—on our ability to think and to function properly. Without a sufficient amount of sleep, we think more slowly. We have trouble making decisions. We make more mistakes and have trouble remembering things. So basically, anything to do with memory, making decisions, thinking—all of these are affected by the lack of sleep. And this is happening to many people. Recent studies show that 40 percent of adults get less than seven hours of sleep each night. So that means four out of ten adults are suffering from sleep deprivation. **E3** So let's talk about the immediate effect of not getting enough sleep, and how it can affect us in every aspect of our lives. For instance, at school. How many of you have stayed up all night to study for a big test? Uh-huh. Well, research shows that in order for us to remember new information, we first need to sleep. It's interesting, right? Sleep assists our memory. So when we sleep, we consolidate and we strengthen our long-term memory. So if you don't sleep enough, learning is harder. In fact, some studies have shown a connection between the amount of sleep students get and their grades in school. Students who get less sleep get lower grades! **E4** Now let's think about work. On the job, sleepy workers cause many workplace accidents. One example is in the medical field. Doctors in hospitals often have to put in long shifts and stay up all night. One recent study looked at doctors who stayed awake all night working thirty-hour shifts. It showed that these tired doctors were seven times more likely to make mistakes on these long shifts than on regular shifts when they got enough sleep. Seven times! These mistakes injured people and even killed patients. **E5** Another place where the immediate effects of sleep deprivation is illustrated is on the road, in car accidents. Did you know that tired drivers cause 20 percent of car accidents in the U.S.? That's about 1,500 deaths and more than 7,000 injuries each year. Many of these accidents occur when tired drivers fall into "micro-sleep," which is falling asleep for several seconds. These people may look awake—their eyes are open—but their brain is asleep. They can't hear anything around them or see anything. It may only happen for a few seconds, but that's long enough to go through a red light, to drive off the highway, or to hit another car. **E6** So, those are all immediate, day-to-day problems caused by when you're trying to function when you're too tired. But there are also long-term consequences of sleep deprivation—especially to our health. For example, there's a link between lack of sleep and weight gain. Studies show that people who get less sleep are more likely to be overweight. When people are tired, they actually get hungrier and eat more than when they're well rested. They also have more time to eat because they're awake. All this adds up to weight gain. In addition, people who get less sleep are more likely to get sick and to have serious health problems. One study concluded that women who sleep less than five hours a night are 40 percent more likely to have heart problems, compared with women who get eight hours of sleep every night. Forty percent—that's a much higher risk! **E7** The scariest thing about sleep deprivation is that most people don't realize that there are dangers! They continue to go to work when they're tired or to drive a car when they're sleepy. And, over time, they may begin to suffer from serious health problems caused by their lack of sleep. But they don't realize the cause. **E8** It's clear we need stronger health education programs to teach people about this problem—to make them realize that they should get enough sleep each night. With more sleep, people will do better at school, be safer at work. And they won't have as many car accidents, and they'll be healthier in the long run. Everyone needs this information. **E9** And that's what I want to look at next, how to educate people about the problem of sleep deprivation. We'll look at one educational program that was recently started . . .

Coaching Tips

[1] **Note-taking: Using charts** The speaker says she's going to talk about two ways sleep deprivation causes problems. Did you hear them? One is the immediate impact. The other is the long-term effects. Here's a tip for setting up your notes: You might make a chart with two columns, one for short-term problems (the immediate impact) and one for long-term problems or effects. Then, as you hear about each type, you can write the information in the correct column. This will make it easy to read your notes later. [2] **Listening: Recognizing new topics** Did you hear the phrase "So let's talk about . . . "? Speakers often use phrases like this to introduce—or signal—new information. When you hear a speaker say, "So let's talk about . . . " or "Let's think about . . . " or "What I want to look at next . . . " be ready for new and important information to follow. [3] **Critical Thinking: Inferencing** The speaker gives an example about sleep deprivation in the medical field. She says that one study shows that doctors working long shifts were seven times more likely to make serious mistakes. Then, she repeats the number: "Seven times!" What does the repetition tell you about this information? What does *how* the speaker says it tell you? [4] **Note-taking: Using abbreviations and symbols** In this lecture, the speaker gives many details. She gives a lot of examples with numbers. You can use abbreviations and symbols to take down information quickly. This will save you time. It'll also save you space, as you can see here: [see video for note-taking example].

Talk about the Topic *page 28*

Molly: That lecture was really good, but I missed a few details. Could we compare notes on some things?

Rob: Sure.

Molly: So, how much sleep does a normal person need? Does anyone have that?

Alana: Uh-huh. She said seven to nine hours, um, so eight hours on average, right?

Ayman: Right. I had a question, too. I wrote down: "Sleep deprivation is a public health issue because it has daily and long-term effects." Is that right?

Rob: Uh-huh, I have that same thing, basically.

Ayman: So that means it affects the public's health, in other words.

Rob: Right. But I think it's also a public health issue because it affects so many people, directly and indirectly.

Ayman: Oh, good point.

Alana: I have a question, too. Can anyone explain the connection between sleep and memory?

Molly: Yeah, I have that in my notes. This is really interesting to me—that in order for people to remember new information, you have to get a full night's sleep. That sleep "consolidates and strengthens" our long-term memories.

Ayman: That means sleep makes our memories stronger.

Rob: Well, sleep doesn't seem to make my memory any stronger.

Ayman: That's because you're sleeping during class!

Rob: Oh ha ha ha.

Take the Unit Test

1. What is the definition of sleep deprivation?
2. What are the effects of sleep deprivation on the brain? Choose *two* answers.
3. How many adults suffer from sleep deprivation?
4. What is an effect of sleep deprivation on students at school?
5. Listen to this excerpt from the lecture. *Well, research shows that in order for us to remember new information, we first need to sleep. It's interesting, right? Sleep assists our memory.* Why does the speaker say, "It's interesting, right?"
6. What happens to tired doctors who work long shifts?
7. How many car accidents in the United States are caused by tired drivers?
8. Why does lack of sleep cause weight gain?
9. What did one study show about women who don't sleep enough?
10. What is the main purpose of the lecture?

Extend the Topic *page 30*

Reporter: And now, in education news: Last year, Central High School changed to a new, later start time. School now begins at 8:30 A.M.—an hour later than it did before. The school made the change because the students weren't getting enough sleep at night.

Principal: The kids used to get up at 6:00 A.M. or even earlier to get to school. We had a big problem with attendance—kids coming in late—and also falling asleep in class.

Reporter: As the school year ends, the school is seeing the results of the change. Attendance is better, with fewer students coming late or calling in sick. Test scores have gone up throughout the school. And car accidents involving teenage drivers have gone down by 16 percent.

Principal: The change has been really positive. Everyone's happier . . . and doing better. It's great.

Build Your Vocabulary *pages 23–24*

A. 1. c 2. a 3. a 4. b 5. a 6. b 7. b 8. a 9. b 10. b
11. a 12. b 13. c **B. Interact with Vocabulary!**
1. from 2. of 3. on 4. up 5. to 6. in 7. in

Focus Your Attention *page 25*

A. 1. First 2. For instance 3. It's clear that

Listen for Main Ideas *page 26*

B. 1. car accidents 2. lower grades 3. mistakes at
work 4. weight gain 5. serious health problems

Listen for Details *pages 26–27*

B. 1. b 2. b 3. a 4. a 5. c 6. a 7. a 8. c 9. a

Talk about the Topic *page 28*

A. 1. Alana, Ayman, Molly 2. Molly (Note: While
it's arguable that all of the students learned
something new, Molly's comment beginning "This
is really interesting . . ." implies that the information
is newly learned.) **B.** Expressing an opinion: 3, 4;
Paraphrasing: 1, 2, 5

Review Your Notes *page 29*

Sleep deprivation: less than 7 hrs of sleep micro-sleep: falling asleep for sev'l seconds		
	Effects	Ex.
brain	can't think/remember	trouble remembering/making decisions
work	make mistakes	doctors injuring/killing patients: 7x more likely
school	learning harder	lower grades
driving	micro-sleep	car accidents: bad drivers cause 20% of accidents—1,500 deaths & 7,000 + injuries/yr
health	problems	wgt gain; heart problems: less than 5 hrs of sleep = women 40% more likely to have

Take the Unit Test

1. a 2. b and c 3. b 4. b 5. a 6. a 7. b 8. a 9. d
10. d

Extend the Topic *page 30*

A. 1. tired students = low attendance, falling asleep
in class 2. start school later

 **TEST** # PUBLIC HEALTH: Sleep

 Listen to each question. Circle the letter of the correct answer.

1. a. getting less than seven hours of sleep a night
   b. feeling tired during the day
   c. falling into micro-sleep
   d. waking up during the night

2. a. strong emotional feelings
   b. trouble making decisions
   c. memory problems
   d. difficulty speaking

3. a. 20 percent
   b. 40 percent
   c. 60 percent
   d. 80 percent

4. a. gaining weight
   b. getting lower grades
   c. having car accidents
   d. making mistakes on the job

5. a. to emphasize an important point
   b. to ask the students' opinions
   c. to give an example
   d. to make a correction

6. a. They are more likely to make mistakes at work.
   b. They can't remember new information.
   c. They have health problems.
   d. They have more car accidents.

7. a. 1,500
   b. 20 percent
   c. a few seconds
   d. 7,000

8. a. People are hungrier and eat more.
   b. People don't go to the doctor.
   c. People fall asleep while driving.
   d. People think they are not tired.

9. a. They are not safe at work.
   b. They are tired all the time.
   c. They gain weight.
   d. They have more heart problems.

10. a. to explain how to get more sleep at night
    b. to explore the effects of sleep deprivation at work
    c. to convince students to change their sleep habits
    d. to show why sleep deprivation is an important public health issue

UNIT OVERVIEW

In this unit, students will explore different approaches to negotiation and learn strategies for successful negotiations. The lecture focuses on a "win-win" approach to negotiation and its benefits. Follow-up projects allow students to role-play negotiations in business or everyday life.

Connect to the Topic *page 32*   *~10 minutes*

As a warm-up activity, consider having students study the three pictures above and talk about what is happening in each (clockwise left to right: negotiating for a new car, negotiating at the produce stand, negotiating in a business meeting). In the introduction, students read a basic definition of *negotiation*. For the survey, students rank different types of negotiation according to their ease/difficulty. They compare their answers with a partner and with the class.

Build Your Vocabulary *pages 33–34*   *~15 minutes*

Students study the following words and phrases related to business and negotiating:

approach	concentrate on	resolve
approaches to	concerned with	success in
avoid	confer	technique
benefits	conflict	to confer with
blames	(to have) conflicts with	to reach an
blames for	fabric	agreement with
circumstances	give in to	(a good) working
concentrate	interrupts	relationship with

For the Interact with Vocabulary! activity, you may want to encourage students to first notice the boldfaced words. Figuring out these collocations can help students more quickly unscramble the sentences.

Focus Your Attention *page 35*   *~10 minutes*

Students learn how lecturers list items in a lecture, such as steps in a process:

There are (three) things . . .
    The first (thing) is . . .
    The second (thing) is . . .

There are (four) steps . . .
    First, . . .
    After . . .
    Now . . .
    Finally, . . .

Listen to the Lecture   pages 36–37   *~30 minutes*

Students indicate what they believe is the most important goal of a successful negotiation (Before You Listen) before listening to the unit lecture on different approaches to business negotiation. They make corrections to incorrect statements based on information from the lecture (Listen for Main Ideas). They also match actions with results of different approaches to negotiation (Listen for Details).
Lecture video time: 6 min. 14 sec.   *Number of episodes: 10*

Talk about the Topic   page 38   *~20 minutes*

Four students—River, Hannah, Mia, and Manny—discuss the lecture. Part A focuses on matching these students with ideas from the discussion. In Part B, your students work on these discussion strategies:

- Asking for opinions or ideas: "Do you guys agree that the 'win-win' approach is best?"
- Expressing an opinion: "I think you should just keep listening, and don't give in."
- Asking for clarification or confirmation: "So you like the hard approach?"

BONUS ACTIVITY

You can supplement this activity by having students compare their opinions with the opinions of the students in the discussion.

For Part C, students are encouraged to use the discussion strategies they've learned. They may use phrases from the student discussion and/or the Discussion Strategy box, or they may come up with their own.
Student discussion video time: 1 min. 13 sec.

Review Your Notes   page 39   *~15 minutes*

Students focus on reconstructing their notes, paying attention to key points discussed in the lecture.

BONUS ACTIVITY

You can supplement this activity by having students use their notes to summarize parts of the lecture with a partner.

Take the Unit Test   *Teacher's Pack page 25*   *~15 minutes*

You may want to play the lecture again just before giving the test. Students answer standard test questions about the content of the lecture. Specifically, the test covers the following: the "hard," "soft," and "win-win" approaches to negotiation, the example discussed in the lecture, and the lecturer's opinion about negotiation.

Extend the Topic   pages 40–41   *~30 minutes*

- Listening and Discussion: Students listen to a TV ad for negotiation training and compare the different negotiations modeled in the ad.
- Project/Presentation: Students create and perform role plays based on situations in business and in everyday life.

Focus Your Attention:
Try It Out! *page 35*

Speaker: Now, it's common for people to have strong emotions during a negotiation, but it's important not to let your feelings hurt the negotiation process. Fortunately, there are a few things you can do to deal with feelings in a negotiation. One thing you can do is to tell each other how you feel. Maybe you're feeling nervous, or even angry about something. The second thing is to listen. Don't talk or argue, just listen. Finally, show some understanding. For example, you may want to say you're sorry, or just say that you understand how they feel. . . .

Listen for Main Ideas and Listen
for Details *pages 36–37*

Business lecturer: **E1** Good morning, everybody. Today I want to talk about negotiation. First, I'd like to talk about why negotiation is so important for business. And then we'll talk about different approaches to negotiation. After that, we'll talk about some techniques for negotiating successfully. **E2** So, why are negotiation skills so important? Every time you need to resolve a problem or reach an agreement with other people, you need to be able to negotiate. We need to negotiate every day with our coworkers, our boss, and people from other businesses. Right? So negotiating is a skill that you will use often as a professional. And knowing how to negotiate well will help ensure your success in business. **E3** The problem is that many people are not very good negotiators. That's because many people perceive only two approaches to negotiation: the hard approach and the soft approach. If you are a hard negotiator, you are concerned with "winning"—with reaching the decision that is best for you. You are not very concerned about the other person or your relationship with that person. Hard negotiators will concentrate on, on getting the decision they want. They won't stop until the other person agrees. In the end, hard negotiators may get what they want. But they may, they may hurt their relationship with the other person, and that person may not want to work with them in the future. **E4** So in contrast, soft negotiators are more concerned with avoiding conflict, avoiding disagreement. They give in quickly because they don't want to have conflict with the other person. This approach to negotiation isn't good because soft negotiators often agree to decisions that are bad for them or bad for their business. Subsequently, they might be unhappy or

disappointed because they believe they've "lost" the negotiation. **E5** So, instead of a hard or a soft approach, successful negotiators like myself take a "win-win" approach, where there isn't a winner or a loser. In the "win-win" approach, negotiators try to confer on a decision—to agree on something that benefits both sides involved. They also try to keep a good working relationship with each other, so they can continue to work together in the future. **E6** So, how do you suppose they can do this? How can you negotiate a solution that is a "win-win" for both people? Well, there are two important techniques that will help you to do this. The first technique is to listen and to understand—to listen and to understand each other's side of the problem. The second technique is to work together to reach a solution—a solution that is good for both people. **E7** Let's look at an example. Imagine you work for a company that makes clothing. To make your clothing, you need to buy fabric from another company. Now let's say you like to buy fabric from Joe because his company makes good fabric and they sell it at a fair price. But, recently you've had a problem. The problem is that Joe's company has been late sending you the fabric that you need. This is causing you problems because then your company can't make your clothing on time. **E8** So, what should you do? The first thing you need to do is to make sure you understand each other's side of the problem. To do that, you need to listen carefully to each other. So first, you should listen carefully to Joe's side of the problem. Joe might say, "Oh, we're having problems with output because the machines at my company are so old" and so on. Don't interrupt him or talk about your side of the problem. Instead, just listen and make sure you understand him. After you have heard and understood the other person, you should explain your circumstances. When you do, don't blame the other person for the problem. If you blame the person, they may get angry and may not want to talk to you anymore. One way to avoid blaming someone is to use "I" statements. That means you start sentences with the word *I* instead of *you*. So don't say to Joe: "You are causing us problems!" That might make Joe angry. Instead you could say, "I am worried because the fabric is late, and we can't make our clothing." This way, you are explaining how you feel, and how the problem affects you. **E9** Now that you've both listened and explained your sides of the problem, you are ready to find a solution together. This step can be difficult because each person may want a different solution. But, instead of arguing for your solution, you should talk about all the possible solutions and then agree on one that is good for both of you. For example, both you and Joe might agree that you will buy some fabric from another company now, and some fabric from Joe's company later. In this solution, you both win because you get the fabric you need now, and Joe can continue to sell you fabric in the future. **E10** So as you can see, if both people in a negotiation try to understand each other and work together, then both of them can "win" and feel happy with the solution.

Coaching Tips

[1] Note-taking: Noting details After the speaker tells the three main ideas of his lecture, he returns to the first idea—the importance of negotiation skills—and gives supporting details. How could you write these details in your notes? Here's one idea: [see video for note-taking example]. **[2] Note-taking: Using symbols** The speaker says that soft negotiators want to avoid conflict. He then says that they do this by "giving in." You can use an arrow (→) to show how these two ideas connect. Using symbols can help you quickly note how ideas are connected. **[3] Critical Thinking: Predicting** The speaker asks, "How can you negotiate a solution that is a 'win-win' for both people?" Try predicting what the speaker will say next. Hint: Did you write down a definition for the win-win approach? If not, listen to that part again, and then use your definition to help you make a prediction. **[4] Listening: Identifying steps in a process** With the rhetorical question "What should you do?" the speaker is about to introduce a list of steps. Listen for words like *First . . .* and *After . . .* and *Now . . . .* These will help you identify the steps as he introduces them. By identifying these signals, you'll be able to record important information in your notes.

Talk about the Topic *page 38*

Manny: There's a lot of different ways to run a business.

Mia: Well, do you guys agree that the "win-win" approach is best? As compared to the soft or hard approach?

Hannah: Well, yeah, I mean, I think it's important that people listen to each other. They have to try to understand each other. It seems like common sense to me.

Manny: Actually, I can't say that I agree with that.

Hannah: Really?

Mia: Really?

Hannah: No?

Manny: No, I mean, we're talking about business. The goal's to make money. To do that, you have to think about yourself.

Hannah: So you like the hard approach?

Manny: Yeah, I guess.

Mia: But if you only think about yourself, no one else will want to work with you. You can't make money alone.

River: But, actually, not everyone you negotiate with is going to take a "win-win" approach. There are a lot of "hard" business people in the world.

Mia: Still, I think you should just keep listening, and don't give in. Keep trying to find other solutions. Eventually, the other person'll agree, if they really want to work with you.

Manny: That seems a little "soft" to me.

Mia: Oh . . .

Take the Unit Test

1. What are hard negotiators concerned about?
2. What is the problem with using the hard approach to negotiation?
3. What do soft negotiators try to do?
4. What is the problem with using a soft approach to negotiation?
5. Listen to this excerpt from the lecture: *So, instead of a hard or a soft approach, successful negotiators like myself take a "win-win" approach, where there isn't a winner or a loser.* What is the speaker suggesting here?
6. Why does the speaker give the example of the clothing factory?
7. What is the purpose for using "I" statements in negotiation?
8. What does the speaker think about getting angry during business negotiations?
9. What are the goals of the win-win approach? Choose *two* answers.
10. What is the speaker's main point about the win-win approach?

Extend the Topic *page 40*

Businessman: I can't believe you lost our order.

Businesswoman: Look, it wasn't my fault. You never sent the order in.

Businessman: Yes, I did. You're to blame for this—and you're going to pay!

Businesswoman: What can I say? We don't need your business, sir. Forget it!

Announcer: Don't let business problems turn into business disasters. Learn to solve problems in a positive way. At Negotiation Solutions, learn to negotiate like a pro. In only four short hours, you'll learn how to turn a lose-lose situation into a win-win.

Businessman: I'm worried because we haven't received our shipment from you yet.

Businesswoman: Let me check . . . No, I don't see an order for you here, sir.

Businessman: Hmm, I'm pretty sure I sent it. It's really important that we get it right away.

Businesswoman: Well, I can put a rush on your order. You'll get it by tomorrow. Will that work?

Businessman: Sure, that'd be great. Thanks so much.
Businesswoman: Anytime.

Announcer: Negotiations Solutions. Learn to negotiate like a pro.

ANSWER KEY

Build Your Vocabulary *pages 33–34*

A. 1. a 2. c 3. b 4. b 5. c 6. a 7. b 8. a 9. c 10. c 11. b 12. **B. Interact with Vocabulary!** 1. different approaches to business negotiations 2. for them to have conflicts with each other 3. to ensure your success in the negotiation process 4. to reach an agreement with the other person 5. to confer with your team members about your decision 6. mostly concerned with making a lot of money
7. concentrate on doing a good job 8. keep a good working relationship with my coworkers. 9. usually give in to my boss 10. my boss for the long hours that I spend at work.

Focus Your Attention *page 35*

A. 1) Tell each other how you feel 2) Listen 3) Show understanding

Listen for Main Ideas *page 36*

B. 1. three approaches 2. makes both people happy 3. fabric company 4. listen to the other side of the problem 5. explain your side and work together to reach a solution

Listen for Details *page 37*

B. 2. c 3. a 4. d 5. h 6. e 7. g 8. f

Talk about the Topic *page 38*

A. *Suggested answers:* 1. Hannah, Mia 2. Manny 3. River **B.** Asking for opinions or ideas: 1; Expressing an opinion: 3, 5; Asking for clarification or confirmation: 2, 4

Review Your Notes *page 39*

Hard	Soft	Win-win
to get your way	to avoid conflict	to find a solution for both sides
Hurt working relationship	Unhappy with outcome	none

1. Understand each other's side: do listen, don't talk
2. Work to find solution: Use "I"; Listen to each other; find solution together

Take the Unit Test

1. d 2. c 3. a 4. d 5. c 6. c 7. b 8. d 9. a and c 10. c

Extend the Topic *page 40*

A. 1. Two businesspeople have a disagreement because an order didn't arrive on time. 2. At first, the people blamed each other and ended their working relationship. Then they agreed on a solution together.

UNIT 4 TEST — BUSINESS: Negotiating for Success

Listen to each question. Circle the letter of the correct answer.

1. a. avoiding conflict
   b. finding a solution that is good for both sides
   c. keeping a good working relationship with the other side
   d. winning the negotiation

2. a. It may be more expensive for both sides.
   b. It may take a long time to find a solution.
   c. You may hurt your working relationship with the other person.
   d. You may not get the solution you want.

3. a. avoid conflict with the other person
   b. change the other person's opinion about the problem
   c. explain the reasons for the conflict
   d. get the best solution for their business

4. a. The negotiation may not be completed.
   b. The other person may not like the solution.
   c. The problem may never be solved.
   d. You may be unhappy with the solution.

5. a. that "win-win" negotiation techniques may not work in all situations
   b. that he enjoys winning negotiations
   c. that he has used "win-win" negotiation techniques in his work
   d. that his students need more experience in negotiation

6. a. to ask for ideas about how to solve the conflict
   b. to describe a problem he had in his business
   c. to illustrate the techniques used in win-win negotiation
   d. to show the problems with an unsuccessful negotiation

7. a. to agree on a solution to the problem
   b. to avoid blaming the other person
   c. to make the other person angry
   d. to understand the other side of the problem

8. a. Getting angry will help you get the decision you want.
   b. People sometimes get angry during negotiations.
   c. Stop negotiating if the other person gets angry.
   d. You cannot negotiate successfully if you make the other person angry.

9. a. finding a solution that works for both sides
   b. getting the decision you want for your business
   c. keeping a good working relationship
   d. reaching a decision quickly

10. a. It is a complicated approach to negotiation.
    b. It is easy to learn the negotiation techniques.
    c. It is the best approach to negotiation.
    d. It is not always successful.

UNIT 5 · ART HISTORY / Modern Art

TEACHING TIPS

UNIT OVERVIEW

In this unit, students will learn about modern art. The lecture contrasts traditional art with modern art. It also defines abstract art and provides examples to illustrate the differences between traditional, realistic art and modern, abstract art. In follow-up projects, students discuss ways to look at art. Then they research and report on an abstract painting.

Connect to the Topic *page 42*   *~10 minutes*

After learning the meaning of the term *modern art*, students look at an abstract painting and choose adjectives that describe it. In small groups, they discuss their opinions about the painting.

Build Your Vocabulary *pages 43–44*   *~15 minutes*

Students study the following words and phrases related to art:

category	the idea of	realistic portrait
category of	image	represented in
communicate	images of	represents
created by	influence on	style
creates	objects	style of painting
different viewpoints	painted with	traditional
emerged	pure	traditional paintings
emerged in	realistic	viewpoint

For the Interact with Vocabulary! activity, you may want to encourage students to first notice the boldfaced words and explain that they form collocations when paired with the correct word.

Focus Your Attention *page 45*   *~10 minutes*

Students learn how speakers provide definitions in a lecture:

What is modern art?
Modern art means . . .
Modern art is . . .

We say this is modern art because . . .
Modern art isn't . . . Instead, it's . . .
How do we define the term modern art?

Listen to the Lecture *pages 46–47*   *~30 minutes*

Students discuss what they like and don't like about three paintings (Before You Listen) before listening to the unit lecture on abstract art. They check words that describe the paintings discussed in the lecture and match key terms with their definitions (Listen for Main Ideas). They also answer true/false questions about details in the lecture (Listen for Details). (Note: If you're having students write out the entire corrected false sentences, you may suggest that students write them in their notebooks because of limited space on the page.)
Lecture video time: 6 min. 52 sec.   *Number of episodes: 9*

26   UNIT 5

> **NOTE**
>
> We recommend that you play the lecture once in "plain" video mode, then once as audio only. For review, you can play the video again with the Presentation Points and/or Coaching Tips turned on. As another review option, students can watch the subtitled version on their own.

Talk about the Topic *page 48*   *~20 minutes*

Four students—May, Qiang, Yhinny, and Michael—discuss the lecture. Part A focuses on matching these students with ideas from the discussion. In Part B, your students work on these discussion strategies:

- Asking for opinions or ideas: "Well, what do you guys think?"
- Agreeing: "I'm like you . . ."
- Disagreeing: "I respect your opinion, but . . ."
- Asking for clarification or confirmation: "Was it a Cubist piece of work? Was it modern art?"

> **BONUS ACTIVITY**
>
> You can supplement this activity by having students compare their opinions to the opinions of the students in the discussion.

For Part C, students are encouraged to use the discussion strategies they've learned. They may use phrases from the student discussion and/or the Discussion Strategy box, or they may come up with their own.
Student discussion video time: 1 min. 15 sec.

Review Your Notes *page 49*   *~15 minutes*

Students focus on reconstructing their notes, paying attention to definitions of key terms and examples discussed in the lecture.

> **BONUS ACTIVITY**
>
> You can supplement this activity by having students use their notes to summarize parts of the lecture with a partner.

Take the Unit Test *Teacher's Pack page 31*   *~15 minutes*

You may want to play the lecture again just before giving the test. Students answer standard test questions about the content of the lecture. Specifically, the test covers the following: traditional art, modern art, representational vs. non-representational art, abstract art, and the three examples of art discussed in the lecture.

Extend the Topic *pages 50–51*   *~30 minutes*

- Listening and Discussion: Students listen to an interview with an art museum guide about ways to look at art. Then they discuss their opinions about abstract art.
- Project/Presentation: Students research a painting and make a presentation to the class.

Focus Your Attention:
Try It Out! *page 45*

Speaker: Now, I'd like to look at more examples. So, we have a portrait. What is a portrait exactly? A portrait is a picture of a person. A portrait can be a painting, photograph, or sculpture that shows a person's appearance . . . what a person looks like. Now, not all paintings with people in them are portraits. You can have a picture with a person in it, and it not be a portrait. Instead, a portrait really focuses on the person, makes the person the center of the picture. Are there any questions? . . .

Listen for Main Ideas and Listen for Details *pages 46–47*

Art history lecturer: E1 Hi everybody. If you remember, in our last class we looked at a painting—an abstract painting—by the Japanese artist Shiraga. Remember that? And a lot of you said, "You know, I just don't get it. I just don't get abstract art." Well, don't worry about it—that's a common feeling. Today, we're going to talk some more about abstract art, so hopefully you'll understand it better. But first, we need to define "modern art" and understand how it's different from "traditional art." Then, under modern art, we'll define "abstract art." And finally, we'll look at two different types of abstract art. OK? E2 So, what is modern art? To many art historians, modern art means the new kinds of art that were created in the twentieth century—in the 1900s, right? Before 1900, most artists created what we call traditional art. Traditional art is both realistic and representational. Representational means that it represents something from the real world—like a person, an object, or a scene in nature. Traditional art also looks realistic. It looks like the person or thing that it represents. Before photography became common in the late 1800s, artists were asked to create realistic paintings of people—or portraits. These were valued because they preserved a person's image. So, as you can see, it was necessary for artists to have the skills to create realistic works of art. E3 Now a famous example of a traditional portrait is one by the Spanish artist Pablo Picasso. He painted his mother in 1896 when he was only fifteen years old. In this painting, Picasso depicts his mother using realistic details and colors, including the color of her skin, her brown hair, and the white dress she was wearing. E4 But even at the time Picasso painted this portrait, the world was changing very quickly. By 1900, many new inventions and new ideas were emerging, and people were looking to the future. So many artists, including Picasso, wanted to create art that was new, that was different from traditional art. So, they started experimenting with new approaches to art. E5 One of these new approaches was called abstract art. So, what exactly is abstract art? Basically, abstract art is art that's not realistic. It doesn't look like anything you see in the real world. There are two main categories of abstract art. The first is representational abstract art. This art represents a person or thing you see in the real world, OK? But we say it is "abstract" because it doesn't look realistic; it changes the way a person or thing looks. So this is called representational abstract art. E6 In the early 1900s Picasso started to experiment with representational abstract art. He and other artists developed a kind of art called "cubism." Now one goal of cubism was to show something from different viewpoints, all at one time. A portrait that Picasso painted of photographer Dora Maar in 1937 demonstrates this style. When you look at this painting—called *The Portrait of Dora Maar*—it looks like Dora has two noses! But in fact, Picasso is presenting two views of Dora's face—one from the side and one from the front. E7 Now, the second category of abstract art is "non-representational abstract art." Unlike representational art, non-representational art doesn't represent anything you see in the real world. Instead, it expresses things you can't see—like ideas or feelings. And another name for this kind of art is "pure abstraction." OK? E8 The first artist to create purely abstract art was a Russian painter named Wassily Kandinsky. Kandinsky created his first purely abstract paintings in 1913. In them he used lines, shapes, and colors to show his feelings. Kandinsky loved music and was even a musician himself. In fact, he said that when he looked at a painting, he could actually hear music. And he wanted to communicate that in his paintings. One of Kandinsky's works is called *Contrasting Sounds*. In it, you can see different lines, shapes, and colors. To Kandinsky, these represented different feelings. For example, in this painting circles are meant to be peaceful shapes. And the contrasting colors, like black and white squares, are meant to represent different sounds, just like in a piece of music. E9 At the time, some people reacted negatively to this art. But, after Kandinsky died in 1944, his work continued to have a major influence on other abstract artists who followed him. And we'll talk about that influence, and other changes in art history, in our next class.

Coaching Tips

[1] Listening: Identifying key terms and definitions Did you hear the definition of *modern art*? Did you understand it? Speakers often introduce key terms and definitions with a question, as the speaker does here with, "So, what is 'modern art'?" Another way speakers signal key terms and definitions is by repeating. Listen again and count how many times the speaker says "modern art." **[2] Listening: Identifying key terms** Did you hear the artist's name? Did you write it in your notes? How did the lecturer signal you this time that she was giving important information? Speakers often pause before they introduce an important—or key— term. In this case, the speaker pauses before she gives the name of a famous artist. **[3] Critical Thinking: Applying knowledge** When you hear "new" information, it's likely you already know something about it. For example, here the speaker defines *abstract art* and *representational abstract art*. Consider what you already know about each of these words: *abstract, art,* and *representational.* Now consider the new definitions you noted. Can you improve the definitions now? **[4] Critical Thinking: Inferencing** In her closing comments, the speaker mentions that some people reacted negatively to Kandinsky's art. Think about the speaker's description of Kandinsky's art and what the speaker said about how the world was changing. Why do you think Kandinsky's work might have been criticized by some?

Talk about the Topic *page 48*

Michael: You want to know what I think? Of all the art that we've talked about today, Kandinsky's is the best, in my opinion. I mean, his style is so much more interesting than traditional art.

Yhinny: Mm. I respect your opinion, but, I mean, his style is sort of strange. Who can tell what he's painted? I mean, only he knows.

Qiang: I'm like you—I'm a traditionalist. I prefer that painting by Picasso, of his mother. Because in that one, you can be sure of what it is.

May: Does anyone remember—was that one . . . I don't know how to say it? Was it a cubist piece of work? Was it modern art?

Qiang: No, I have that Picasso was still in his traditional period—it was in the late 1800s. He was just fifteen years old.

Michael: Well, what do you guys think? Like, OK, traditional is fine. But imagine how boring the art world would be if that's all we had to look at.

May: Oh yeah.

Yhinny: I wouldn't be bored. Maybe I still don't "get" abstract art. But, I mean, do you really hear music when you look at something like Kandinsky's *Contrasting Sounds*?

May: I kind of do.

Yhinny: Oh!

May: Really! I don't know it does something to me. I don't know how to say it. Is that strange?

Michael: No.

Qiang: No, makes sense.

Yhinny: Kind of. It is.

Take the Unit Test

1. What kind of art was made before 1900?
2. What is a representational painting?
3. Why does the speaker include the portrait of Picasso's mother in the lecture?
4. What event in the early 1900s influenced the development of abstract art?
5. Which painting is an example of cubism?
6. Why did Picasso paint two noses in the *Portrait of Dora Maar*?
7. What do artists try to express in "pure" abstraction?
8. How did Kandinsky show his ideas in his paintings?
9. Listen to this excerpt from the lecture: *At the time, some people reacted negatively to this art. But, after Kandinsky died in 1944, his work continued to have a major influence on other abstract artists who followed him.* What can you infer about Kandinsky and his art? Choose *two* answers.
10. What is the speaker's main purpose in the lecture?

Extend the Topic *page 50*

Art museum guide: How should you look at abstract art? That's a question that many people ask. Well, take some time to just look at the painting. Look at it from different viewpoints. You do this by first standing back. Looking at the painting from far away. Then come closer and see how it changes. Next think: What kind of impact does the painting have on you? How does it make you feel? Some abstract paintings seem happy and bright, while others feel sad and heavy. Think about why the painting makes you feel that way. OK, then notice the colors. Are they bright, happy colors, or dark, serious colors? Also look at the shapes in the painting. Are they big and obvious, or small and detailed? Is the painting full of action, or is it very simple? By noticing all of these things, you'll be able to see a painting in a new and different way every time you look at it!

Build Your Vocabulary *pages 43–44*

A. 1. b 2. a 3. d 4. c 5. h 6. f 7. g 8. e 9. l 10. j
11. i 12. k **B. Interact with Vocabulary!** 1. by
2. in 3. realistic 4. different 5. of 6. in 7. on
8. with 9. of 10. painting 11. of 12. traditional

Focus Your Attention *page 45*

A. a person; photograph; person

Listen for Main Ideas *pages 46–47*

B. *Maria Picasso Lopez, the Artist's Mother*:
portrait, representational, realistic; *Portrait of Dora
Maar*: portrait, representational, abstract, cubism;
Contrasting Sounds: abstract, non-representational,
pure abstraction **C.** c, b, a

Listen for Details *page 47*

B. 1. F (twentieth century) 2. F (fifteen years old)
3. T 4. F (example of representational abstract
art/cubism) 5. T 6. F (in 1913) 7. F (to represent
different feelings) 8. T

Talk about the Topic *page 48*

A. *Suggested answers*: 1. May, Michael 2. Qiang,
Yhinny 3. Yhinny **B.** Asking for opinions or ideas:
4, 6; Agreeing: 2, 5; Disagreeing: 1; Asking for
clarification or confirmation: 3

Review Your Notes *page 49*

modern art	art created in the 20th century	Picasso's *Portrait of Dora Maar*, Kandinsky's *Contrasting Sounds*, Shiraga's paintings
representational	stands for something from the real world	Picasso's *Maria Picasso Lopez, the Artist's Mother*
realistic	looks like something from the real world	Picasso's *Maria Picasso Lopez, the Artist's Mother*
abstract	not realistic	Picasso's *Portrait of Dora Maar*
cubism	style of abstract art	Picasso's *Portrait of Dora Maar*
non-representational	doesn't represent anything you see in the real world	Kandinsky's *Contrasting Sounds*
pure abstraction	another name for non-representational	Kandinsky's *Contrasting Sounds*

Take the Unit Test

1. a 2. a 3. b 4. d 5. c 6. a 7. c 8. d 9. c and d
10. a

Extend the Topic *page 50*

A. 2, 3, 5

UNIT 5 **TEST** # ART HISTORY: Modern Art

Listen to each question. Circle the letter of the correct answer.

1. a. traditional art
   b. modern art
   c. Cubism
   d. pure abstraction

2. a. a painting that shows an image from the real world
   b. a painting that has bright colors
   c. a painting that shows something from different viewpoints
   d. a painting that does not look realistic

3. a. to explain how Picasso used color in his painting
   b. to give an example of a traditional painting
   c. to prove that Picasso was a great painter
   d. to show a painting that she likes

4. a. New types of paint were being invented.
   b. Artists were earning a lot of money selling abstract paintings.
   c. Many artists were moving to Europe to paint.
   d. The world was changing and many new ideas were emerging.

5. a. *Untitled*, by Shiraga
   b. *Maria Picasso Lopez, the Artist's Mother*, by Picasso
   c. *Portrait of Dora Maar*, by Picasso
   d. *Contrasting Sounds*, by Kandinsky

6. a. He wanted to show Dora Maar's face from two different viewpoints.
   b. He thought Dora Maar was ugly.
   c. He made a mistake when he was painting.
   d. He wanted to paint an unusual painting.

7. a. the way things really look
   b. bright colors
   c. ideas and feelings
   d. people and objects from the real world

8. a. by listening to music
   b. by adding letters and words
   c. by showing how things really look
   d. by using lines, colors, and shapes

9. a. He sold a lot of paintings during his lifetime.
   b. He was influenced by Picasso's style of painting.
   c. Other artists got ideas from his paintings.
   d. Some people did not like his paintings.

10. a. to define different styles of art
    b. to give an opinion about the best kind of art
    c. to give examples of successful artists
    d. to tell the story of Pablo Picasso's life

UNIT 6 TECHNOLOGY Robots

TEACHING TIPS

UNIT OVERVIEW

In this unit, students will learn about the history of robots and other machines. The lecture provides a basic definition of the term *robot*. It also provides a history of robots, ending with an overview of the main types of robots used today. In follow-up projects, students research and report on other robots in use today.

Connect to the Topic *page 52*   *~10 minutes*

Students are introduced to the term *robot* through a variety of photos (clockwise from left to right: an exploring robot, the robot Asimo, an assembly line, a robotic vacuum, computer-controlled cameras). In the survey, students brainstorm lists of jobs that robots can and can't perform, then share their lists with the class.

Build Your Vocabulary *pages 53–54*   *~15 minutes*

Students study the following words and phrases related to technology and robots:

automatically	industry	powered by
constructed	mechanical	programmed
creator of	nuclear	programmed for
designed	obtain	significant
designed by	obtained by	significant to
dull	performed by	task
explore	pick up	used in
get information from		

For the Interact with Vocabulary! activity, you may want to encourage students to first notice the boldfaced words and explain that the boldfaced words form collocations when paired correctly.

Focus Your Attention *page 55*   *~10 minutes*

Students learn how to listen for and write down numbers that they hear in lectures. For example, they learn to distinguish between numbers such as *13* and *30*. They also listen for large numbers and for years.

> **BONUS ACTIVITY**
>
> You can supplement this activity by dictating numbers and years to students as they listen and write the numbers. Alternatively, students could dictate numbers to each other in pairs.

Listen to the Lecture *pages 56–57*   *~30 minutes*

Students consider what they know about robots (Before You Listen) before listening to the
unit lecture on robots. They number pictures based on the order in which they are mentioned
in the lecture (Listen for Main Ideas) and answer multiple-choice questions about details
(Listen for Details).
Lecture video time: 5 min. 56 sec.   *Number of episodes: 11*

Talk about the Topic *page 58*   *~20 minutes*

Four students—Alana, Rob, Molly, and Ayman—discuss the lecture. Part A focuses on
matching these students with ideas from the discussion. In Part B, your students work on
these discussion strategies:

- Offering a fact or example: "And we learned that a robot has to have senses—you know,
  like it can feel, like even smell, or see . . . "
- Trying to reach a consensus: "So, anything else? . . . "

BONUS ACTIVITY

You can supplement this activity by having students compare their opinions with the
opinions of the students in the discussion.

For Part C, students are encouraged to use the discussion strategies they've learned. They may
use phrases from the student discussion and/or the Discussion Strategy box, or they may
come up with their own.
Student discussion video time: 1 min. 27 sec.

Review Your Notes *page 59*   *~15 minutes*

Students focus on reconstructing their notes, paying attention to the definition of *robot* and
the tasks a robot can do. They also reconstruct details about the examples of robots mentioned
in the lecture.

BONUS ACTIVITY

You can supplement this activity by having students use their notes to summarize parts of
the lecture with a partner.

Take the Unit Test *Teacher's Pack page 37*   *~15 minutes*

You may want to play the lecture again just before giving the test. Students answer standard
test questions about the content of the lecture. Specifically, the test covers the following: the
definition of *robot*, the history of robots, what modern robots need to do, and how robots are
used.

Extend the Topic *pages 60–61*   *~30 minutes*

- Listening and Discussion: Students listen to a news report about a research study done
  with a robotic dog. Then they discuss their opinions about using robots as companions.
- Project/Presentation: Students research a robot not mentioned in the lecture and make a
  presentation to the class.

Focus Your Attention:
Try It Out! *page 55*

Speaker: Now I want to talk about a recent robotic car competition. Beginning in 2004, teams of scientists from all over the world have met once a year for a robotic car competition. In this competition, all of the cars are robots—meaning they have no drivers. In 2007, the competition was held in a city, where the cars raced for 60 miles over city streets. Thirty-five teams entered cars in the race, hoping to win the $2 million prize for first place. The first place car traveled at only 14 miles per hour, but still finished about twenty minutes before the second place car. All right, is everyone with me so far? . . .

Listen for Main Ideas and Listen for Details *pages 56–57*

Technology lecturer: E1 OK, let's get started. First, I'd like to review a basic definition of *robot*. Then we'll look at some examples of robots in history. And finally, we'll look at how robots are being used today. E2 One simple way to define *robot* is to say it's a machine, a mechanism that can move automatically, or by itself. Many people think a robot needs to look or think like a human, but as you'll see in my examples, that's not always true. Sometimes robots look like people, but not always. OK? E3 Now let's look at some robots through history. You may think that the idea of robots is new, but actually people have imagined robots for a really long time. Thousands of years ago, the ancient Greeks wrote stories about robots. These robots included mechanical people made of gold and tables that could walk around by themselves. Around 400 BCE—that's about 2,400 years ago—a Greek mathematician named Archytas designed and built a real robot, a mechanical bird that he called "the pigeon." The pigeon was powered by steam and it could actually fly, though not very far. In 1495, Leonardo da Vinci, the famous Italian artist and inventor, designed the first human-like robot. This robot was a knight. In da Vinci's drawings, the knight could sit up and move its arms and legs and head like a human. However, we don't know if he ever actually constructed this robot. E4 Then, in 1898, Nikola Tesla created the first radio-controlled robot. Tesla was a famous scientist from Croatia who worked on many inventions, including the first radio. His robot was a boat that was powered by a battery. When people first saw Tesla's boat moving by itself, they thought he was controlling it with his

mind. But he was actually controlling it with radio signals. E5 Finally, in the late 1940s, something very significant happened: the computer. Since the 1940s, scientists have been able to use computers to make robots that can be programmed—that can be controlled by a computer "brain." The first programmable robot was created in, in 1954 by George Devol. Devol's an American inventor who created some of the first robots to be used in industry, in factories. E6 So, today, robots are programmable; they're controlled by computers. And today's robots must be able to do two things in general: First, they have to be able to obtain information from their environment. That means robots need to have "senses"—they have to be able to see and feel, hear, or even smell and taste things. E7 And then, they need to do something with that information—perform a task, like pick up an object and move it. For example, a robot used in a car factory might be programmed by a computer to "see" a car part in front of it. And then it can pick up that part and connect it to another part of the car. E8 Today, robots do lots of work for people, and most of that work is what we call "the three Ds"— dull, dirty, and dangerous. In other words, most robots do work for people that people don't either want to do or they can't do. The main way that we use robots today is in industry, mostly in factories. And in fact, 90 percent of the robots in use today are in factories. Now, robots are very useful in factories because they can do work that is very dull—very boring. They can do the same task again and again and again—without getting tired or bored. For example, chocolate factory robots pick up chocolates and put them into boxes. It's impossible for a person to do a task like this as well as a robot. I mean, a robot can do this 20,000 times in one eight-hour workday. Twenty thousand times! I don't think any of us could do that. Robots are also used in industry to perform work that is too dirty or dangerous for humans, such as cleaning up nuclear waste. E9 A second way that robots are used is in exploration. Robots are used to explore and get information from places that are dangerous or impossible for people to visit. For example, robots are used to explore volcanoes where it's very hot and unsafe. Or in Antarctica where it's very cold. And robots are also very important for exploring other planets, like Mars. These exploring robots are able to take pictures and gather information so that we can learn more about these places without actually going there. E10 Robots are also becoming more common for personal use. Many people use robots to vacuum their homes or as toys just to play with. In 2004, about 2 million personal robots were used worldwide, and that number has continued to go up. For instance, the government of South Korea hopes to have a personal robot in every Korean home by the year 2013. And now scientists are working on robots that can drive our cars for us, or take care of us when we are sick or old, or just be our friends. Now, that's an interesting thought, isn't it? **E11** So, that's a brief history of robots, and some examples of how we use robots today. For the next time, I'd like you to imagine what kind of robots we'll be using in the future.

Coaching Tips

[1] Listening: Recognizing numbers Because this lecture is, in part, about history, the speaker will be giving a lot of dates. It's important for you to understand these numbers so that you can note them correctly. For example, if the year is *1495* (one-four-nine-five), you'll hear *fourteen ninety-five*. Four-digit years are typically said in two halves like this.

[2] Note-taking: Adding visuals The speaker tells you about Archytas and his pigeon powered by steam. Can you imagine what that might have looked like? How it worked? Visualizing or drawing things that a speaker describes is a good practice for better remembering information from a lecture.

[3] Note-taking: Using graphic organizers The speaker gives several examples of robots in this lecture. With each example, he provides details to help you understand how the robot works or what it does. Noting information in a graphic organizer like this one can help make relationships clearer in your mind: [see video for note-taking example].

[4] Critical Thinking: Responding to a topic How do you feel about the idea of a robot taking care of you when you're sick or older? In a lecture, if you have a reaction to information you hear, write your thoughts in the margin of your notes. When you review your notes later, this note will help you connect to—and remember—this part of the lecture.

Talk about the Topic *page 58*

Molly: So, could we review the basic definition of a robot?

Rob: Sure.

Alana: Well, there are a lot of different kinds of robots, right? Like those in factories.

Rob: Well, right, but, now what makes something a robot? You know? Like, one, it has to be something that's controlled by a computer.

Ayman: And we learned that a robot has to have senses—you know . . .

Rob: Oh yeah!

Ayman: . . . like it can feel, even smell, or see.

Molly: Yeah—I thought that was so interesting how some robots can even "taste."

Rob: Yeah!

Ayman: Right, but the definition is they have to be able to obtain information from the environment . . .

Molly: . . . through their "senses."

Ayman: Exactly.

Molly: Yeah.

Rob: So, what else?

Alana: Mmm, I wrote down that they have to be able to do a job, like pick something up and move it.

Molly: That means "perform a task."

Ayman: Task?

Rob: Task. T-a-s-k.

Ayman: Oh, right.

Molly: All right, so anything else? Great. Well, that's our basic definition!

Rob: All right, then. Do you want to move on to talk about the idea of robots for personal use? Like, for example, I think the idea of a robot being used to care for somebody that's old or sick is sad. I think that's really sad. I think a person should do that.

Molly: Yeah.

Ayman: Yeah, I'm with you. But you know, I would love to have my own robot, you know? To clean my room or fix me dinner.

Alana: Or take tomorrow's quiz for us!

Rob: Right.

Molly: Exactly.

Take the Unit Test

1. What is the lecture mainly about?
2. What is the simple definition of a robot?
3. When was the first robot built?
4. What kind of robot did Leonardo da Vinci design?
5. What did Tesla's radio-controlled robot look like?
6. What is a programmable robot?
7. What do modern programmable robots need to do? Choose *two* answers.
8. Where are most robots used today?
9. Where are robots used for exploration? Choose *two* answers.
10. Listen to this excerpt from the lecture: *And now scientists are working on robots that can drive our cars for us, or take care of us when we are sick or old, or just be our friends. Now, that's an interesting thought, isn't it?* What is the speaker suggesting here?

Extend the Topic *page 60*

Radio reporter: Psychologists have known for some time that older people who live alone feel happier if they have a pet or are visited by a pet, such as a cat or a dog. In a recent study, university researchers tested out this idea. They compared two groups of older people. All of them lived alone. The people in the first group were visited every week by a real dog named Sparky. The people in the second group were visited by a robotic dog name AIBO. Each dog visited with each older person for thirty minutes every week. The dogs sat with the people and kept them company. Both wagged their tails and let the people pet them. The surprising part is that after eight weeks, *both* groups felt happier and less lonely. The researchers say this means that someday robots may not only help us, but they may also become our companions.

ANSWER KEY

Build Your Vocabulary *pages 53–54*

A. 1. d 2. c 3. f 4. a 5. e 6. b 7. i 8. j 9. g 10. l
11. k 12. h **B. Interact with Vocabulary!** 1. d 2. a
3. e 4. b 5. c 6. h 7. j 8. f 9. i 10. g

Focus Your Attention *page 55*

A. Beginning <u>2004</u>; <u>2007</u>—cars raced: <u>60</u> miles, <u>35</u> teams, <u>$2 mil.</u> prize; 1st place: <u>14</u> mph, finished <u>20</u> min.

Listen for Main Ideas *page 56*

B. 1. Archytas, creator of a mechanical bird 2. da Vinci's robot sketch 3. Tesla's radio-controlled boat
4. industrial robot 5. exploring robot 6. personal robot

Listen for Details *page 57*

B. 1. b 2. b 3. b 4. a 5. a 6. c 7. b 8. a 9. c 10. a

Talk about the Topic *page 58*

A. *Suggested answers* 1. Rob, Molly, Ayman
2. Rob, Molly, Ayman 3. Alana, Rob, Molly, Ayman
B. Offering a fact or example: 1, 2, 3; Trying to reach a consensus: 4, 5

Review Your Notes *page 59*

def. of robot: A machine that can move by itself;
2 things a robot can do: 1) obtain information
2) perform a task: dull: same task again and again, like in a chocolate factory; dirty: cleaning up nuclear waste; dangerous: exploring volcanoes, Antarctica, Mars

	Created in:	Use/ability:
Archytas's pigeon	**400** BCE	could fly—not far
da Vinci's knight	1495	**drawing only; could move/sit up**
Tesla's boat	**1898**	**radio-controlled**
Industrial robot	**in use today**	**factories**
Exploring robot	**in use today**	**explore volcanoes, planets (like Mars), Antarctica**
Personal robot	**in use today**	**friend/companion; vacuum**

Take the Unit Test

1. d 2. b 3. a 4. d 5. b 6. c 7. b and d 8. b
9. b and d 10. b

Extend the Topic *page 60*

A. Sparky group: 1, 2, 4, 5; AIBO group: 1, 3, 4, 5

UNIT 6 TEST TECHNOLOGY: Robots

Listen to each question. Circle the letter of the correct answer.

1. a. how to build a robot
   b. ideas about robots in ancient times
   c. robots in industry
   d. the history of robots

2. a. a machine that can do dangerous work
   b. a machine that can move automatically
   c. a machine that can think
   d. a machine that looks like a person

3. a. about 2,400 years ago
   b. about 2,000 years ago
   c. about 400 years ago
   d. about 200 years ago

4. a. a robot that could draw
   b. a robot that could fight
   c. a robot that could fly
   d. a robot that looked like a human

5. a. a bird
   b. a boat
   c. a knight
   d. a walking table

6. a. a robot that can do boring jobs
   b. a robot that can talk
   c. a robot that is controlled by a computer
   d. a robot that is used in industry

7. a. communicate with other robots
   b. get information from the environment
   c. make decisions
   d. perform a task

8. a. at home
   b. in industry
   c. in schools
   d. in the military

9. a. in the ocean
   b. in outer space
   c. in medicine
   d. in volcanoes

10. a. that these types of robots exist today
    b. that these types of robots could change our lives
    c. that these types of robots are dangerous
    d. that these types of robots are difficult to design

MEDIA STUDIES
Video Games

UNIT OVERVIEW

In this unit, students will discuss various types of media and the pros and cons of using each. The lecture explores the pros and cons of children playing video games. In follow-up projects, students debate the use of media such as television, video games, and the Internet.

Connect to the Topic   *page 62*   *~10 minutes*

As a warm-up activity, consider asking students to identify which medium is represented in each photo (newspaper, radio, Internet). In the introduction, students are exposed to the following terms: *media, electronic, pros,* and *cons.* Then they survey each other on the types of media they use and the amount of time they spend using them. They discuss their results with the class.

Build Your Vocabulary   *pages 63–64*   *~15 minutes*

Students study the following words and phrases related to media studies and video games:

affected by	connection between	intellectual
affects	development	interaction between
aggressive	disagreement about	interactions
attention spans	effects	issues
behavior	effects on	makes up
behavior in	evidence	prevents from
concern	get along with	violent
concerned about	grades	

For the Interact with Vocabulary! activity, you may want to encourage students to first notice the boldfaced words. Figuring out these collocations can help students more quickly unscramble the sentences.

Focus Your Attention   *page 65*   *~10 minutes*

Students learn cues that lecturers use to explain opinions and to present evidence supporting different sides of an issue:

One side of an issue:	**Reasons or evidence:**	**Another side of an issue:**
Critics worry/think . . .	*. . . because . . .*	*But . . .*
Some argue/think . . .	*This is because . . .*	*However, . . .*
Another concern . . .	*In fact, . . .*	*Others think . . .*
Critics say . . .	*Studies show . . .*	*On the other hand, . . .*
According to . . .	*Research shows . . .*	
	One survey found . . .	

Listen to the Lecture *pages 66–67*

Students consider what is good and bad about children's playing video games (Before You Listen) before listening to the unit lecture on the pros and cons of video game use. They complete an outline of the lecture's main ideas, guided by three topic headings. (Listen for Main Ideas). Then they answer true/false questions based on details from the lecture (Listen for Details).

Lecture video time: 6 min. 25 sec.   *Number of episodes: 9*

Talk about the Topic *page 68*

~20 minutes

Four students—Yhinny, Michael, May, and Qiang—discuss the lecture. Part A focuses on matching these students with ideas from the discussion. In Part B, your students work on these discussion strategies:

- Disagreeing: "Wait. I don't think the lecturer said that, exactly."
- Paraphrasing: "She said the evidence only shows a connection between violent games and aggressive children."

BONUS ACTIVITY

You can supplement this activity by having students compare their opinions with the opinions of the students in the lecture.

For Part C, students are encouraged to use the discussion strategies they've learned. They may use phrases from the student discussion and/or the Discussion Strategy box, or they may come up with their own.

Student discussion video time: 1 min. 34 sec.

Review Your Notes *page 69*

~15 minutes

Students focus on reconstructing their notes, paying attention to the effects of video games on children's development, including both concerns and research findings.

BONUS ACTIVITY

You can supplement this activity by having students use their notes to summarize parts of the lecture with a partner.

Take the Unit Test *Teacher's Pack page 43*

~15 minutes

You may want to play the lecture again just before giving the test. Students answer standard test questions about the content of the lecture. Specifically, the test covers the following: the number of children who play video games and the positive and negative effects of video games on children.

Extend the Topic *pages 70–71*

~30 minutes

- Listening and Discussion: Students listen to a TV show in which a host and guest debate Internet use by teenagers.
- Project/Presentation: Students choose a medium, such as television, video games, or the Internet, and have a debate about its use.

Focus Your Attention:
Try It Out! *page 65*

Speaker: Now, there are different points of view on the effects of video games on children. Many critics say that video games have negative effects on children, that they're bad for them. But others feel that video games are not all bad, and that in fact, games can have positive effects on children and teach them some useful skills. First, let's take a look at the negative effects. One concern is that video games are bad for children's health. This is because to play most games, children sit still and don't get any exercise. On the other hand, research shows that video games are good for children's vision—their ability to see. Video games can also help children develop good hand-eye coordination—the ability to react or respond quickly to something they see. So, we have two points of view . . .

Listen for Main Ideas and Listen for Details *pages 66–67*

Media studies lecturer: E1 In this class we've already studied a variety of media. And remember, by "media" we mean different ways that we communicate—such as newspapers, television, and movies. Today we're going to talk about another kind of media—electronic games—that is, video and computer games. Let's see a show of hands: How many of you grew up playing these kinds of games on your game systems or computers? **E2** All right, then it'll come to no surprise that in the last thirty years, these games have become one of the most popular forms of new media, especially with children. Now, as these games have gotten more popular, some people have become concerned about their effects on children. As a result, in recent years many studies have been done on the effects of video games. Today, we'll look at some of that research and talk about some of the effects—positive and negative—of video games on the children who play them. **E3** But first, how many children do you think play video games? Any idea? Well, one recent survey found that 87 percent of eight- to seventeen-year-olds in the U.S. play video games. Pretty common, right? Another study found that thirteen-year-old boys spend an average of twenty-three hours a week playing video games, while thirteen-year-old girls spend about twelve hours a week. That's a lot of time playing games, isn't it? **E4** So, as I said, some are concerned about how this affects kids. One of the main concerns is the effect on kids' social development—their ability to get along with

other people. Another worry is the effect on their intellectual development—their ability to think and learn. So, let's take a closer look at those two areas. **E5** First, social development. We know that interaction with other children is very important for social development. Many people worry that children who play video games a lot are spending too much time alone. Critics say that kids should be playing with other kids—interacting and learning to get along with others. They say that playing video games is anti-social. But research seems to show that the opposite is true, that playing video games often is a social activity. One study found that 60 percent of game players play with friends. It turns out, then, that video games may not be as anti-social as some critics thought. **E6** Another concern about video games is that a lot of them are violent, and that playing violent games will teach children to be violent. We do know that some popular games contain a lot of violence, like shooting and fighting. For example, *Grand Theft Auto* is a game that is very well known for its violence. And we also know that children who play violent games are more likely to be aggressive. For example, a study of thirteen- and fourteen-year-olds found that those who played violent games were more likely to argue with their teachers and to get into fights. But there really isn't enough proof—or evidence—to say for sure that video games cause this aggressive behavior because many of these studies only show a connection between violent games and aggressive behavior. In other words, aggressive kids may choose to play violent games. It's not clear that the games make them aggressive. **E7** OK, those are the social development issues. Now, let's look at video games' effect on children's intellectual development. Some argue that because video games are full of action that changes quickly, children don't learn to concentrate on things for very long. They say games cause children to develop short attention spans. Critics also say that many games don't allow children to think creatively—to think of new ideas—because they just follow the story of the video game. They don't make up their own stories. For these reasons, many people are concerned that video games can hurt children's ability to think and learn. And actually some studies have shown that children who play a lot of video games do have poorer grades in school. **E8** However, other research shows that not all video games are bad for children's intellectual development. In fact, good video games can help children learn. This is because children learn best when they're entertained, when they're having fun. Today, many games not only entertain, but also require players to be creative and use problem-solving skills to win the game. **E9** Well, as we've learned, there is a lot of disagreement about the effects of video games on children. But it's clear that video games are not going away, so we need to keep creating good video games. Next time, I'd like to talk more about games that are good for children.

Coaching Tips

[1] Listening: Reviewing Sometimes a speaker will begin a lecture by reminding everyone of a key word or idea learned in a past lecture. Here the speaker revisits the word *media*, reminds everyone of the definition, and gives examples of different types of media. This quick review makes it easier to connect what you already know to the new information you will hear. **[2] Note-taking: Using charts** The speaker says she'll be talking about two effects: positive and negative. At this time you may want to create a chart in your notes, showing two columns: one for listing positive effects and the other for listing negative effects. It might look something like this: [see video for note-taking example].
[3] Listening: Recognizing contrast Be aware of words that signal contrasting information. Sentences beginning with *But . . .*, *However . . .*, or *On the other hand . . .* often go on to introduce another side of an issue. You just heard the opinion that video games are anti-social. What would be the contrasting view of that? Write down your thoughts, then listen to what the lecturer says. **[4] Critical Thinking: Identifying point of view** Throughout the lecture, the speaker offers facts and opinions from different viewpoints. Based on the lecturer's presentation, what can you guess about her opinion on video games? Why do you think this? Now consider your own opinion.

Talk about the Topic *page 68*

Qiang: So, it seems that video games aren't so bad for you!

Yhinny: Wait. I don't think the lecturer said that, exactly.

Qiang: No? She didn't?

Yhinny: No, not exactly. It depends on the game and how much of it you play, isn't that what she said?

Michael: Yeah.

Qiang: Well, I don't play much now, but when I was younger, I used to play for hours every day. And now, I consider myself normal.

Michael: Uh, well, that's your opinion.

Qiang: Ah, come on.

May: So wait, did you say that you played violent video games as a kid? Because I personally don't think parents should let their children play those kinds of games.

Qiang: No, no—I agree with you on that. I played mostly sports video games. Or one of those silly adventure games.

Michael: Really, it's unfair to completely blame the video games. I mean, she said the evidence only shows a connection between violent games and aggressive children. But it's not cause and effect, remember?

Qiang: Wait. Can you say that again?

Michael: OK, so there's a connection between violent games and aggressiveness. But it's not cause and effect. Violent games don't cause violent behavior.

Yhinny: Good point. I think a kid's already aggressive, and maybe that's why he or she likes aggressive games.

May: It's true. It's, it's kind of like that whole expression. What, what is it—the, "the chicken or the egg"?

Qiang: Hey, "Chicken and Egg"! That sounds like a good name for a video game—an educational video game, of course!

Yhinny: Silly!

Take the Unit Test

1. What is the main purpose of the lecture?
2. Which of these effects of video game playing does the lecture discuss? Choose *two* answers.
3. What percentage of eight- to seventeen-year-old children play video games in the United States?
4. What type of child spends twenty-three hours a week playing video games?
5. What fact does the speaker give to show that playing video games can be a social activity?
6. What is the connection between violent video games and aggressive behavior?
7. How can video games help children learn? Chose *two* answers.
8. Which is true about children who play a lot of video games?
9. The speaker talks about all of the following negative effects of video game playing *except* which one?
10. Listen to this excerpt from the lecture: *Well, as we've learned, there is a lot of disagreement about the effects of video games on children. But it's clear that video games are not going away, so we need to keep creating good video games.* What is the speaker's attitude about video games?

Extend the Topic *page 70*

Bob: So, 70 to 90 percent of teenagers use the Internet. They're using it to send messages to each other, talk in chat rooms, and just search the Web. So what's wrong with that? Well, look at the information teenagers can get on the Web. So much of it is just bad for kids—violent and dangerous.

And then there are the strangers that teens can meet online. It's just not safe.

Guest: Well, face it, Bob: The Internet is here to stay whether you like it or not, and I think you're forgetting the positives. Yes, there is dangerous information online, but parents need to control the sites that their kids look at, and teach them how to avoid dangerous situations. Actually, there's also a lot of good information on the Web that can help kids learn. In fact, some research shows that using the Internet helps teens to read better and get better grades in school.

Bob: Well then, my question is . . . What is my question? . . .

ANSWER KEY

Build Your Vocabulary *pages 63–64*

A. 1. a 2. a 3. a 4. b 5. a 6. b 7. a 8. b 9. a 10. b 11. b 12. a **B. Interact with Vocabulary!**
1. concerned about the kind of media that children use 2. disagreement about the effects of television on children 3. negative effects on kids' social development 4. aggressive behavior in children 5. children to get along with others 6. a connection between violent TV shows and aggressive behavior 7. watching TV prevents children from thinking creatively 8. affected by what they see on TV 9. interaction between students 10. make up their own stories and be creative (*or* be creative and make up their own stories)

Focus Your Attention *page 65*

A. Negative: 1. Bad for children's health because they sit still; Positive: 1. = ability to see 2. = ability to react/respond quickly to something

Listen for Main Ideas *page 66*

B. 1. e 2. d 3. g 4. a 5. c

Listen for Details *page 67*

B. 1. F (87 percent) 2. T 3. T 4. F (evidence only shows a connection) 5. F (teach children to think creatively and use problem-solving skills) 6. F (some have lower grades) 7. T 8. T

Talk about the Topic *page 68*

A. *Suggested answers:* 1. May, Qiang 2. Yhinny, Michael, May **B.** Disagreeing: 1, 3; Paraphrasing: 2, 4

Review Your Notes *page 69*

social development concerns: ability to get along with others, may become violent; **social development research:** 60% play with friends; violent gamers are aggressive; **intellectual development concerns:** ability to think, learn, concentrate, be creative; **intellectual development research:** some gamers have poorer grades in school; good games can help students learn

Take the Unit Test

1. b 2. c and d 3. c 4. a 5. b 6. b 7. b and c 8. d 9. b 10. c

Extend the Topic *page 70*

A. 1. His attitude is negative. He's concerned that teenagers spend too much time on the Internet, and it's dangerous. 2. She feels that the Internet has positive aspects and can be useful. She mentions that using the Internet may help teens read better and get better grades.

 **MEDIA STUDIES: Video Games**

 Listen to each question. Circle the letter of the correct answer.

1. a. to compare two popular types of video games

   b. to describe the positive and negative effects of video games

   c. to explain how to make good video games

   d. to give examples of violent video games

2. a. effects on health

   b. effects on family relationships

   c. effects on intellectual development

   d. effects on social development

3. a. 67 percent

   b. 77 percent

   c. 87 percent

   d. 97 percent

4. a. boys

   b. children from wealthy families

   c. children who do poorly in school

   d. older children

5. a. Thirteen-year-old boys spend twenty-three hours a week playing video games.

   b. Sixty percent of children play video games with friends.

   c. Kids who play violent video games are more likely to get into fights.

   d. Many video games require players to be creative.

6. a. Violent video games cause aggressive behavior in children.

   b. Children who play violent games are more likely to be aggressive.

   c. Children may play violent video games instead of fighting with each other.

   d. There is no connection between violent video games and aggressive behavior.

7. a. Children can learn at their own speed.

   b. Children learn better when they have fun.

   c. Some video games teach problem-solving skills.

   d. Video games help children learn about technology.

8. a. They are more likely to be overweight.

   b. They don't like playing with other children.

   c. They argue a lot with their parents.

   d. They get poor grades in school.

9. a. It may hurt children's ability to learn.

   b. It may hurt children's language abilities.

   c. It may make children become anti-social.

   d. It may make children more aggressive.

10. a. She belives that children should not be allowed to play them.

   b. She thinks that parents should buy more video games for their children.

   c. She sees their popularity as a chance to make them better.

   d. She thinks that there are no good video games.

UNIT 8 BIOLOGY
Genetically Modified Food

TEACHING TIPS

UNIT OVERVIEW

In this unit, students will learn about genetic modification and genetically modified (GM) food. The lecture looks at three types of genetic modification in food. In follow-up projects, students discuss food labeling and conduct a survey outside of class to learn people's attitudes toward GM food.

Connect to the Topic *page 72*   *~10 minutes*

As a warm-up activity, ask students to look at the cartoon and explain what's humorous about it. In the introduction, students are exposed to the concept of genetically modified food and are given a definition of *gene*. In the survey, they give their opinions about the genetic modification of food and the use of chemicals on crops. They share their answers in groups.

Build Your Vocabulary *pages 73–74*   *~15 minutes*

Students study the following words and phrases related to biology and GM food:

bacteria	made a purchase	retain
common bacteria	modify	retain their flavor
consume	modify genes	solve problems
consumed by insects	normal	source
crops	pesticide	source of vitamins
genetically modified food	picks	stays fresh
grow crops	primarily	(the) use of pesticides
just picked fruit	purchase	vitamins

For the Interact with Vocabulary! activity, you may want to encourage students to first notice the boldfaced words and explain that they form collocations when paired with the correct word.

Focus Your Attention *page 75*   *~10 minutes*

Students learn cues that speakers use to introduce important key terms in a lecture:

emphasizing the term by saying it louder or longer   *spelling the term*
repeating the term   *making a hand gesture that goes with the term*
pausing before and/or after the term   *writing the term on the board*

Listen to the Lecture *pages 76–77*   *~30 minutes*

Students guess what the speaker's opinion of GM food will be (Before You Listen) before listening to the unit lecture on genetically modified food. They match types of food with the reasons they were developed (Listen for Main Ideas), and then answer true/false questions about the details in the lecture (Listen for Details).
Lecture video time: 6 min. 22 sec.   *Number of episodes: 11*

Talk about the Topic   page 78

~20 minutes

Four students—May, Qiang, Yhinny, and Michael—discuss the lecture. Part A focuses on matching these students with ideas from the discussion. In Part B, your students work on these discussion strategies:

- Offering a fact or example: "There are a lot of governments that won't even let these foods come into their countries."
- Keeping the discussion on topic: "Let's get back to our notes."
- Trying to reach a consensus: "OK. Maybe we should just 'agree to disagree' on this one?"

For Part C, students are encouraged to use the discussion strategies they've learned. They may use phrases from the student discussion and/or the Discussion Strategy box, or they may come up with their own.
Student discussion video time: 1 min. 21 sec.

Review Your Notes   page 79

~15 minutes

Students focus on reconstructing their notes, paying attention to details about the three types of GM food discussed in the lecture.

Take the Unit Test   *Teacher's Pack page 49*

~15 minutes

You may want to play the lecture again just before giving the test. Students answer standard test questions about the content of the lecture. Specifically, the test covers the following: the speaker's attitude about GM food and the three examples of GM food discussed in the lecture.

Extend the Topic   pages 80–81

~30 minutes

- Listening and Discussion: Students listen to and discuss a radio report about labeling requirements for GM foods in different countries.
- Project/Presentation: Students work in groups to conduct surveys outside of class to gather people's opinions on GM food. They report their findings and conclusions to the class.

Focus Your Attention:
Try It Out! *page 75*

Speaker: Today, we're going to talk about the genetic modification of food. That's genetic modification: g-e-n-e-t-i-c. Genetic modification. Genetic modification is when scientists change the genes inside a living thing, like a plant or animal. These changes make the plant or animal grow in a different way. Another term for this type of food is transgenic food. That's transgenic: t-r-a-n-s-g-e-n-i-c. Transgenic food. So that's what we're going to look at today. Before we go on, though . . .

Listen for Main Ideas and Listen
for Details *pages 76–77*

Biology lecturer: E1 All right my friends, today we're going to continue with our discussion of genetic modification. Now, does everyone remember our definition? Yes? No? We're not sure. OK, let's recap. Genetic modification is when we change the genes inside of a living thing to make it grow in a different way, OK? All right. Today, we're going to talk specifically about genetically modified food—or GM food, for short. Genetic modification has produced many new possibilities in plant biology. Scientists have been able to create all kinds of new plants, and it's really a very exciting time in this field. But there are some people who are against this practice, and we'll talk more about that later.
E2 Right now, we're going to look at three types of genetic modification: first, modifications to make food stay fresh longer; second, modifications to make crops grow better; and third, modifications to make food healthier. **E3** Our first example is about a modification made to help food retain freshness longer. It was called the FlavrSavr Tomato. That's spelled F-l-a-v-r-S-a-v-r, FlavrSavr. And like the name says, it was supposed to save the flavor of a fresh tomato. Now it's interesting actually because it was the first genetically modified food to be sold in U.S. supermarkets, back in 1994. **E4** So, why was this tomato created? Well, there's a big problem with growing fruits and vegetables, and that's keeping them fresh. Like tomatoes: After you pick them, they go bad quickly. They get too soft, they don't taste good anymore. Now, the reason the tomato goes bad is because of a special chemical inside the tomato plant. This chemical starts to work after a tomato is picked, starts making it get soft.
E5 Scientists wanted to stop this chemical from working. To do this, they created the FlavrSavr Tomato by adding a gene called antisense RNA.

That's a-n-t-i-s-e-n-s-e. Antisense. This antisense RNA gene stops the chemical that makes tomatoes get soft. The chemical doesn't function, so the tomato stays fresh for a long time, much longer than a normal tomato. **E6** But there were some problems with the FlavrSavr Tomato. One problem was that people didn't trust this new genetically modified food. They thought it might be unhealthy or even dangerous to eat, so they didn't buy it. Another problem was that, well, people said it just didn't taste very good. At any rate, shoppers didn't purchase the FlavrSavr, so it wasn't grown anymore after 1997. **E7** Our next example is a plant that was developed to grow more easily, a type of corn called Bt Corn. That's B-t Corn. Now, all farmers have problems with insects eating their crops. And corn farmers have problems with an insect called a rootworm. This worm gets inside the corn plant and it eats it. And these worms can kill an entire corn crop. For a long time, the only method for getting rid of these insects was the use of pesticides. But, as you know, pesticides cause problems, too, because, while they do kill pests, they also can be dangerous to people and the environment. And they're very expensive to use. So it isn't the best solution to the problem. And this is why Bt Corn was developed. **E8** To make Bt Corn, scientists used a common bacteria called the Bt bacteria. This bacteria lives in the ground and makes a natural poison that kills insects. But it doesn't hurt people at all. So scientists added the Bt gene to corn plants, and now when insects consume the plant, they die, but people and animals aren't hurt at all. Now for farmers, Bt Corn is one of the most popular genetically modified crops today. It's grown all over the world, although the corn is used primarily as food for animals.
E9 Finally, let's look at a food that's been created to solve a health problem. Millions of people around the world—the poorest people—they don't get enough food with vitamin A—you know, the, the vitamin in orange foods like carrots and sweet potatoes. And this causes serious health problems: Over a million children die each year from a lack of vitamin A, and another 300,000 go blind. So scientists thought if they could add vitamin A to rice, it would help millions of people eat better and live healthier lives. They came up with a new kind of rice with extra vitamin A in it. It's called Golden Rice. **E10** To make Golden Rice, scientists took a vitamin A gene from a plant—a daffodil, which is a flower—and added this gene to the rice plant. Looking at the rice, it looks just like regular rice, except it has a kind of a yellowish-orange, golden color—like a carrot. That's the vitamin A gene giving it that orange color. At this point, Golden Rice is still being studied to make sure it's safe. So it's being grown in a few places, as a part of these studies, but we'll have to see if it becomes a

common source of vitamin A in the future. E11 So that gives you some ideas of the three main reasons why genetically modified plants have been developed. Next time we're going to look at exactly how this works in more detail.

Coaching Tips

[1] Note-taking: Organizing main ideas How many types of genetic modification will you hear about? In your notes, think about creating three areas—maybe three columns—one for each type of modification. It's a good idea to leave a lot of space so that you can write information about each type of modification. Here's one look: [see video for note-taking example]. **[2] Listening: Identifying key terms** Did you write down the name of the gene that keeps the FlavrSavr Tomato fresh longer? What told you that the term was important enough to write down? Maybe you understood its importance from the way the lecturer presented it. He spoke slowly, spelled it out, and repeated it. A speaker might also pause before giving a key term, say it loudly, or use hand gestures. From these cues, you can guess that the term is important. **[3] Critical Thinking: Guessing** Can you think of a solution to the rootworm problem the speaker describes? Maybe think about what scientists did to solve the tomato problem. When you make guesses about something, you prepare yourself for the information or answers that are about to be presented. **[4] Note-taking: Reviewing** Quick: Can you name the three main reasons? What about the example that went with each modification? One good way to review the main points of a lecture is to review your notes with a classmate. This way you'll develop a better understanding of the lecture and have a chance to improve your notes. *And* you'll have fun doing it!

Talk about the Topic *page 78*

May: I don't know about everyone else, but I personally don't trust genetically modified foods.

Michael: I agree. I don't trust them either. I mean, me, I won't buy GM foods. In fact, there are a lot of governments that won't even let these foods come into their countries.

Qiang: Hmm, that's a strong reaction, in my opinion. Don't you think? I mean, look at Bt Corn—it takes away the need for pesticides. Isn't that a good thing?

May: It's so unnatural, and it would never happen in nature. What, a gene's suddenly in a corn plant and it poisons insects? Come on. It's really strange.

Michael: Yeah, and besides, big business is behind all of these products. I mean, they just want to make a lot of money off of all of this.

May: Uh-huh. Exactly!

Qiang: Actually, I don't disagree with you on that point. I mean, food is a big business, and of course the food companies [are] trying to make their money on it. Right?

Yhinny: Overall, I agree with Qiang. I can't understand why people have such big fears about GM foods. If we can produce healthier foods, why not do it?

Michael: OK. Maybe we should just "agree to disagree" on this one?

Qiang: Sure.

May: No problem.

Yhinny: Fine! Agreed!

Qiang: Let's talk about something else.

Michael: Thank you!

May: Let's get back to our notes.

Take the Unit Test

1. Listen to this excerpt from the lecture: *Genetic modification has produced many new possibilities in plant biology. Scientists have been able to create all kinds of new plants, and it's really a very exciting time in this field. But there are some people who are against this practice, and we'll talk more about that later.* What is the speaker's attitude about creating genetically modified food?
2. Why was the FlavrSavr Tomato developed?
3. Why did consumers stop buying FlavrSavr Tomatoes? Choose *two* reasons.
4. Why was Bt Corn developed?
5. What is the problem with using pesticides to kill insects?
6. Where does the Bt gene come from?
7. Why was Golden Rice developed?
8. Who can be helped by Golden Rice?
9. Where does Golden Rice get its color?
10. What is this lecture mainly about?

Extend the Topic *page 80*

Radio reporter: The label on a package of food can show many things. It can show the ingredients that are used to make the food. It can also list information on the amount of vitamins or fat in a food. But should food labels show if the food comes from genetically modified crops? Currently, Japan and countries in the European Union have strong labeling requirements. Labels must include information about any genetically modified ingredients. But many countries do not require labeling—including the United States and Argentina, where most of the world's GM crops are grown. Many consumers want labeling so that they can choose not to eat GM food—for safety or other reasons. However, many people in the food industry say that labeling is not necessary. They say that GM food is safe, and consumers shouldn't worry about it. This week we'll be featuring . . .

ANSWER KEY

Build Your Vocabulary *pages 73–74*
A. 1. b 2. c 3. a 4. b 5. a 6. c 7. a 8. c 9. b 10. b
11. a 12. c B. **Interact with Vocabulary!**
1. Genetically 2. modify 3. solve 4. common
5. picked 6. stays 7. use 8. consumed 9. grow
10. source 11. made 12. flavor

Focus Your Attention *page 75*
Today: genetic modification; Also called:
transgenic food

Listen for Main Ideas *page 76*
B. 1. d 2. a 3. c

Listen for Details *page 77*
B. 1. F, T, F, F 2. T, T, F, T 3. F, T, T, F

Talk about the Topic *page 78*
A. *Suggested answers:* 1. May, Michael 2. Qiang,
Yhinny 3. May, Qiang, Michael B. Offering a fact
or example: 1, 2; Keeping the discussion on topic:
4; Trying to reach a consensus: 3

Review Your Notes *page 79*

	FlavrSavr Tomato	Bt Corn	Golden Rice
Developed?	stays fresh longer	to resist insects	to help w/health (blindness) due to lack of vitamin A
How modified?	added antisense gene to	added bacteria	added daffodil gene
What modification does:	stops chemical	kills insects	includes vitamin A
# of people using today?	0	farmers around the world	in experimentation
other:	people didn't like flavor/ didn't trust	mostly for animals	(Could assign students to research status)

Take the Unit Test
1. a 2. d 3. b and d 4. c 5. a 6. a 7. d 8. c 9. d
10. a

Extend the Topic *page 80*
A. Check: Japan, European Union

 **BIOLOGY: Genetically Modified Food**

 Listen to each question. Circle the letter of the correct answer.

1. a. He thinks it is a good idea.
   b. He doesn't have an opinion about it.
   c. He wants to stop it.
   d. He thinks scientists should be more careful.

2. a. to have a redder color
   b. to have a better flavor
   c. to kill insects that eat tomato plants
   d. to stay fresh longer

3. a. They thought they were too expensive.
   b. They were worried about safety.
   c. The tomatoes didn't stay fresh in the store.
   d. The tomatoes didn't taste good.

4. a. to be healthier for people to eat
   b. to grow in cold weather
   c. to kill insects that eat corn crops
   d. to taste better

5. a. They are dangerous and expensive.
   b. They are difficult to use.
   c. They don't work well.
   d. They kill the corn crop.

6. a. a bacteria that lives in the dirt
   b. a chemical pesticide
   c. an insect that eats corn
   d. the inside of a corn plant

7. a. to grow a stronger rice plant
   b. to kill insects that eat rice plants
   c. to make rice look good when it's cooked
   d. to solve a health problem

8. a. doctors in poor countries
   b. farmers who grow rice
   c. millions of children around the world
   d. scientists who create genetically modified food

9. a. from a bacteria
   b. from carrots
   c. from the way it's cooked
   d. from vitamin A

10. a. different types of genetically modified food
    b. the dangers of genetically modified food
    c. the history of genetically modified food
    d. the scientists who make genetically modified food

UNIT 9 — ASTRONOMY: The Search for Extraterrestrial Intelligence

TEACHING TIPS

UNIT OVERVIEW

In this unit, students will discuss the possibility of life on other planets. The lecture focuses on the SETI (Search for Extraterrestrial Intelligence) Project. In follow-up projects, students work in groups to discuss items they would send into space to represent life on Earth.

Connect to the Topic *page 82*   *~10 minutes*

Students are introduced to the terms *astronomy* and *extraterrestrial*. They respond to statements about extraterrestrial life, then share their opinions in small groups.

Build Your Vocabulary *pages 83–84*   *~15 minutes*

Students study the following words and phrases related to astronomy and the SETI Project:

all over the world	in the universe	searching for
assume	intentionally	sequence
billion	light years	signal
communicate with	listening for	spaceships
conditions for life	located	technology
estimate	number of	travel at
galaxy	on Earth	travel by
	project	

After the Interact with Vocabulary! activity, you may want to have students practice using the boldfaced words with their partners. Knowing collocations can help students expand their vocabularies and increase their fluency.

Focus Your Attention *page 85*   *~10 minutes*

Students learn cues that lecturers use to express how certain they are about ideas or information (degrees of certainty):

Facts:	Theories:	Possibilities:
Mars is the fourth planet . . .	*It's very probable that . . .*	*Maybe . . .*
In 1965, the spaceship	*It's likely that . . .*	*There may/could be . . .*
Mariner 4 . . .	*It makes sense that . . .*	*It's possible that . . .*
	We assume that . . .	*We think that . . .*

Listen to the Lecture *pages 86–87*   *~30 minutes*

Students make guesses about the SETI Project (Before You Listen) before listening to the unit lecture on the SETI Project. They answer multiple-choice questions about the main ideas (Listen for Main Ideas) and about the details of the lecture (Listen for Details).

Lecture video time: 6 min. 7 sec.   Number of episodes: 8

Talk about the Topic   *page 88*

~20 minutes

Four students—River, Hannah, Manny, and Mia—discuss the lecture. Part A focuses on matching these students with comments or ideas from the discussion. In Part B, your students work on these discussion strategies:

- Asking for opinions or ideas: "Let's imagine we've received a signal from aliens. What happens next?"
- Expressing an opinion: "Excuse me, but I have difficulty believing that aliens exist."
- Offering a fact or example: "You heard about that spaceship crash that happened in Roswell, New Mexico, right?"

BONUS ACTIVITY

You can supplement this activity by having students compare their opinions with the opinions of the students in the discussion.

For Part C, students are encouraged to use the discussion strategies they've learned. They may use phrases from the student discussion or they may come up with their own.
Student discussion video time: 1 min. 15 sec.

Review Your Notes   *page 89*

~15 minutes

Students focus on reconstructing their notes, paying attention to facts, theories, and possibilities discussed in the lecture.

BONUS ACTIVITY

You can supplement this activity by having students use their notes to summarize parts of the lecture with a partner.

Take the Unit Test   *Teacher's Pack page 55*

~15 minutes

We suggest you play the lecture again just before giving the test. Students answer standard test questions about the content of the lecture. The test covers the following: why scientists believe there may be life on other planets, how they are searching for other intelligent life, and the SETI Project.

Extend the Topic   *pages 90–91*

~30 minutes

- Listening and Discussion: Students listen to and discuss a talk show monologue about communicating with extraterrestrials.
- Project/Presentation: Students work in groups to decide on a list of ten things they think would represent life on Earth to aliens. They present their lists to the class and explain the reasons for their choices.

Focus Your Attention: Try It Out! *page 85*

Speaker: OK, moving on. Scientists at NASA think there could be water on the planet Mars. A spaceship flying around Mars took pictures of the planet. The pictures show marks on the planet that look like dry rivers. Now, we don't know how old the rivers are. They could be only a few hundred years old, or they could be millions of years old. However, if there were water, it seems very probable that there was some kind of life on Mars at one time. But we assume that there is no life there now. Let's see, now, how many of you . . .

Listen for Main Ideas and Listen for Details *pages 86–87*

Astronomy lecturer: E1 Hello, everyone. Today, we're going to talk about one of my favorite areas of research, the SETI Project—or the Search for Extraterrestrial Intelligence. The SETI Project is a worldwide effort by scientists to look for signals from other intelligent beings in the universe. And it's fascinating to me because the project explores what people have always wondered: Is there anyone else out there? And if so, are they trying to communicate with us? E2 I'd like to examine this more closely, and I'm going to start with a couple of questions: First, why do so many of us assume that there are other intelligent beings in the universe? And second, if there really are, how can we find them? Let's talk first about this assumption that there must be intelligent life. Is there anyone else out there? Well, first let's think about our planet Earth. We have life on this planet because we have the right conditions. We have sun that gives us heat. And we have water, which every living being requires. And as a result, over a long time, intelligent life has developed here—although sometimes we don't seem all that intelligent. E3 Anyway, now think of all the stars in the night sky. Each star that you see could be a sun like our sun, with planets around it. In our galaxy—the Milky Way—there are an estimated 200 billion stars, at least. Two hundred billion! Wow. And, throughout the universe—which is all of outer space—there are at least 100 billion other galaxies. You do the math: That's billions and billions of stars. And maybe one of those stars somewhere in another galaxy is like our sun. And maybe that sun has a planet like our Earth, with the right conditions for life to develop. Right? And maybe intelligent life has developed, and those beings, just like us, are wondering, is there anyone out there? So, this is really an assumption about numbers. With the huge number of stars in the universe, it seems very probable, very likely, that somewhere out there, there is other intelligent life. E4 But then the next question is, if there are these intelligent beings out there, how are they going to communicate with us? In popular culture—in movies and TV—the aliens always arrive in a spaceship, right? But actually, that would be very difficult. For one thing, the universe is really, really big, and spaceships just don't travel very fast. Take, for example, the star Alpha Centauri in the Milky Way. It's 4.2 light years away. If we used our fastest rockets, it would take us 60,000 years to reach Alpha Centauri. Who's got that kind of time? E5 So, traveling here by spaceship would take way too long. But think about it. When you want to visit someone far away, do you just jump in a plane and fly over there? No, you e-mail, or you text them; you give them a call first, right? Or don't you? So it makes much more sense, if these aliens want to communicate, they won't just travel all the way here to Earth. They'll give us a call first. So assuming that there are intelligent beings out there, trying to communicate with us, trying to give us a call, how do we look for their signal? What do we look for? Well, the SETI search looks for radio signals coming from outer space. They use large radio telescopes, located all over the world, to listen for these signals. These telescopes look like big, round dishes and work like a big, giant ear, listening to signals from outer space. E6 So we are making another assumption here, that the aliens will communicate with us by radio signals. OK, but why radio signals? First, because the technology to make radio signals is not very complicated. We've had radio signal technology for more than a hundred years, so we're assuming that other beings probably have this technology as well. Second, there's the speed of radio signals. They travel at the fastest speed in the universe, the speed of light. So, imagine this: If radio signals were sent from Alpha Centauri, they'd get here in almost four years. And that's a lot faster than the 60,000 years a spaceship would take. E7 So, OK. We have these radio telescopes, and we're listening. But what are we listening for? I mean, are we waiting for the aliens to send a voicemail saying, you know, "Hello? Anybody home?" Well, no. We're not listening for something like that. We aren't even listening for words or language. Instead, we're looking for a very strong signal that stands out, and that is different from other signals in space. It has a series or a sequence of signals showing some kind of order. We assume that if a signal is very strong and in a series or a sequence, that it's being sent intentionally, sent by someone. Then we'll pay attention, and we'll listen some more, and try and find out who is sending it and what it means. **E8** Now here's really something to think about: What happens if we find a signal that we think is from aliens? This is something the scientists at the SETI Project have planned for.

Coaching Tips

[1] Listening: Recognizing irrelevant details The speaker says, "Intelligent life has developed here—although sometimes we don't seem all that intelligent." Is this detail important for understanding the lecture? Or does the speaker say it just to make you laugh? You can guess from the fact that she smiles, the students smile, and the speaker moves quickly on to her next point that this is a joke and not something you need to make note of.

[2] Critical Thinking: Inferencing Based on what the speaker has said about the probability of the existence of extraterrestrials, how do you think she'd feel about contact with other intelligent life? Think about her assumptions, for example. Through inference, you can expand your understanding of a topic. **[3] Critical Thinking: Predicting** Have you noticed that the speaker often introduces the next point in the lecture with a question? By answering the questions to yourself, you can predict what's coming next. In this case, what might the answer be? By thinking about possible answers, you prepare yourself to receive new information. **[4] Note-taking and Listening: Degrees of certainty** The speaker gives information about the speed of radio signals. In your opinion, is this information a fact, theory, or possibility? It's good to understand how certain an idea is. In your notes, you can show which items are facts, theories, or possibility by making a chart like this one: [see video for note-taking example].

Talk about the Topic *page 88*

Mia: Hey, let's imagine we've received a signal from aliens.

Manny: That'd be so cool.

Mia: What happens next? Think about it. I mean, it would really change all of our lives, wouldn't it?

River: Yeah, no doubt about it. How exciting—and scary—to discover extraterrestrial life!

Mia: Well, what would happen if they did make contact? Would we signal back to them?

Manny: Why yes, of course. If we didn't, they'd just think, "Nobody's home," and contact another planet.

Hannah: Excuse me, but I have difficulty believing that aliens exist. I mean, they would've contacted us by now. Right?

River: Well, maybe they've tried, and we just haven't been able to read their signals.

Hannah: I suppose that's a possibility.

Manny: Actually, I believe it's already happened. In fact, you heard about that spaceship crash that happened in Roswell, New Mexico, right?

Mia: That's a good story.

River: Some people believe aliens landed in a small town in southwestern United States in the late 1940s.

Hannah: What? You don't believe that, do you? Why would you believe that?

Manny: I read it on the Internet.

Mia: You know you can't believe everything you read on the Internet.

River: But this blogger cited Wikipedia.

Take the Unit Test

1. Which topics are discussed in the lecture? Choose *two* answers.
2. What conditions are necessary for developing life on other planets?
3. About how many stars are in the universe?
4. Why do scientists assume that there is other intelligent life in the universe?
5. How many years would it take for a radio signal to travel from Alpha Centauri to Earth?
6. Listen to this excerpt from the lecture: *When you want to visit someone far away, do you just jump in a plane and fly over there? No, you e-mail, or you text them; you give them a call first, right? Or don't you? So it makes much more sense, if these aliens want to communicate, they won't just travel all the way here to Earth. They'll give us a call first.* What point is the speaker making with this example?
7. Where are SETI's radio telescopes located?
8. Which is *not* a reason why aliens will communicate with us by radio signal?
9. What kind of signal are SETI scientists searching for?
10. What is the speaker's attitude about the SETI Project?

Extend the Topic *page 90*

Talk show host: And did you hear about the Beatles song they sent into space? Yeah, a Beatles song. It's the fiftieth anniversary of the first U.S. space mission—when the U.S. sent the *Explorer 1* satellite into space, in 1958. So, to celebrate our fifty years in space, what does NASA do? They send a Beatles song, "Across the Universe," into space. They sent it toward the star Polaris—the North Star—which is 431 light years away. That means the song won't even reach Polaris for 431 years! But did you know that actually, the Earth has been sending out noise pollution into space for the past 80 years—ever since radio was invented? I didn't realize that. So all the radio signals and TV signals and satellite signals have been floating out into space all this time. So maybe, by the time the Beatles song gets there, the aliens will be, like, "Will you be quiet!? Turn down your radio!!" Who knows? . . .

ANSWER KEY

Build Your Vocabulary *pages 83–84*

A. 1. c 2. a 3. b 4. c 5. b 6. a 7. c 8. a 9. b 10. c 11. b 12. a **B. Interact with Vocabulary!** 1. for 2. with 3. in 4. of 5. by 6. for 7. at 8. over 9. on 10. for

Focus Your Attention *page 85*

A. NASA scientists: there could be <u>water</u> on the planet Mars (Theory/Possibility); spaceship took pictures <u>of the planet</u> (Fact); probable: some kind of <u>life</u> on Mars (Theory/Possibility); assume no life there now (Theory/Possibility)

Listen for Main Ideas *pages 86–87*

B. 1. b 2. a 3. b 4. b

Listen for Details *page 87*

B. 1. a 2. b 3. a 4. b 5. a 6. a 7. a 8. b

Talk about the Topic *page 88*

A. *Suggested answers:* 1. River, Mia 2. Manny
B. Asking for opinions or ideas: 1, 2; Expressing an opinion: 3; Offering a fact or example: 4

Review Your Notes *page 89*

Facts	Theories/Possibilities
Conditions that support life include sun and water.	There are billions of stars, one of which might have a planet like Earth, with the right conditions (sun and water) for life.
The universe is big. Spaceships don't travel fast enough.	Aliens have spaceships like ours. Aliens wouldn't just show up.
Radio signal technology is fast and simple.	Aliens will believe it's easier to signal than to visit. Aliens have radio signal technology.

Take the Unit Test

1. a and d 2. d 3. d 4. a 5. b 6. d 7. a 8. d 9. c 10. a

Extend the Topic *page 90*

A. 1. 50 2. 431 3. 80

ASTRONOMY: The Search for Extraterrestrial Intelligence

 Listen to each question. Circle the letter of the correct answer.

1. a. how scientists search for other intelligent life in the universe
   b. when scientists started searching for other intelligent life in the universe
   c. where in the universe scientists are searching for other intelligent life
   d. why scientists think there may be other intelligent life in the universe

2. a. air and water
   b. heat and air
   c. sunlight and clouds
   d. water and sunlight

3. a. 60 billion
   b. 100 billion
   c. 200 billion
   d. billions and billions

4. a. because there are so many other planets in the universe
   b. because they have received signals from other planets
   c. because alien spaceships have come to Earth
   d. because people have seen aliens in space

5. a. 4.2
   b. 4
   c. 200
   d. 60,000

6. a. that aliens don't have the ability to travel to Earth
   b. that she doesn't visit her friends very often
   c. that the aliens probably live very far away
   d. that aliens probably would search the universe in the same way as humans

7. a. all over the world
   b. in North America
   c. in space
   d. on the ocean

8. a. It takes a long time for spaceships to travel to Earth.
   b. Radio signals travel very fast.
   c. Radio technology isn't complicated.
   d. We are sending radio signals into space.

9. a. a long, loud signal
   b. a signal with words or language
   c. a signal with a strong sequence
   d. a very fast signal

10. a. She believes there probably is intelligent life somewhere in the universe.
    b. She doubts that scientists will find any intelligent life in the universe.
    c. She feels there are better ways to search for intelligent life in the universe.
    d. She thinks that aliens have already visited Earth.

TEACHING TIPS

UNIT OVERVIEW

In this unit, students will learn about Sir Ernest Shackleton's journey to Antarctica in 1914 on his ship the *Endurance*. The lecture describes this journey and survival story, focusing on Shackleton's leadership skills and efforts to save his crew. In follow-up projects, students learn about other explorers and adventurers and report their findings to the class.

Connect to the Topic *page 92*   *~10 minutes*

As a warm-up activity, consider having students look at the photos and captions and share what else they know about these explorers/adventurers and why they're historic. For the survey, students work in groups to rank a list of qualities needed for crew members on an expedition to Antarctica. They present and explain their choices to the class.

Build Your Vocabulary *pages 93–94*   *~15 minutes*

Students study the following words and phrases related to history and Shackleton's journey:

credited	keep up	sailed
credited with	leadership	sank
crew	loyal	sank under
crushed	loyal to	showed signs of
depressed	morale	stuck
exploration of	ordered	stuck in
finally	remembered as a	survived
gave the order	hero	survived by
goal	rescued	team
interact with	rescued by boat	treat with respect
jobs	respect	worked together

After the Interact with Vocabulary! activity, students may practice the boldfaced collocations with partners.

Focus Your Attention *page 95*   *~10 minutes*

Students learn cues that lecturers use to express chronological order. Students also practice using abbreviations for dates and expressions of time such as the following:

10/2/1914   *~ 5 days*
1/1915   *< 1 wk.*
1916   *> 3 hrs.*
10 mos.

BONUS ACTIVITY

You can supplement this activity by dictating dates, years, and other time expressions. Students listen and write the dates and time expressions they hear. Alternatively, students could dictate dates and time expressions to each other in pairs.

Listen to the Lecture *pages 96–97*   *~30 minutes*

Students make guesses about Shackleton's journey (Before You Listen) before listening to the unit lecture on Shackleton's journey to Antarctica. They complete a timeline with dates and times mentioned in the lecture (Listen for Main Ideas). Then they answer true/false questions based on details in the lecture (Listen for Details).

Lecture video time: 6 min. 22 sec.   *Number of episodes: 11*

BONUS ACTIVITY

You can supplement the Listen for Details activity by having students change the false statements to true statements.

Talk about the Topic *page 98*   *~20 minutes*

Four students—Mia, Manny, Hannah, and River—discuss the lecture. Part A focuses on matching these students with comments or ideas from the discussion. In Part B, your students work on these discussion strategies:

- Asking for opinions or ideas: "Yeah, so, I'm curious about everyone's thoughts . . ."
- Expressing an opinion: "Wow! That was a great story!"
- Keeping the discussion on topic: "Guys, I think we're supposed to be talking about the lecture we heard today."

BONUS ACTIVITY

You can supplement this activity by having students compare their opinions with the opinions of the students in the discussion.

For Part C, students are encouraged to use the discussion strategies they've learned. They may use phrases from the student discussion and/or the Discussion Strategy box, or they may come up with their own.

Student discussion video time: 1 min. 30 sec.

Review Your Notes *page 99*   *~ 15 minutes*

Students focus on reconstructing their notes, paying attention to important dates and events in the story of Shackleton's journey.

Take the Unit Test *Teacher's Pack page 61*   *~ 15 minutes*

You may want to play the lecture again just before giving the test. Students answer standard test questions about the content of the lecture. Specifically, the test covers the following: the goal of Shackleton's trip, Shackleton's leadership skills, and the main events of the journey.

Extend the Topic *pages 100–101*   *~30 minutes*

- Listening and Discussion: Students listen to and discuss a report on the flight of the *Apollo 13* space mission.
- Project/Presentation: Students research other explorers and adventurers and report their findings to the class.

Focus Your Attention:
Try It Out! *page 95*

Speaker: This time, we're going to talk about Ernest Shackleton and his trip on the ship the *Endurance*. The *Endurance* left London on August 1, 1914. It took them over four months to reach the Antarctic Circle. First, they sailed to Buenos Aires, Argentina, where they picked up more men for their crew. They left Buenos Aires on October 26 and stopped at a whaling station in South Georgia—a place where whaling boats stopped while hunting whales in the Atlantic Ocean. This was the last stop before Antarctica where any people lived. So on December fifth, the crew said good-bye to the people at the whaling station and sailed toward Antarctica. It was the last time they would see any other people for quite some time . . .

Listen for Main Ideas and Listen
for Details *pages 96–97*

History lecturer: **E1** When we think of the great explorers, we typically remember them for achieving their goals, right? But today I'm going to tell you the story of Sir Ernest Shackleton and his trip to Antarctica. Now his goal was to lead the first group to cross Antarctica on foot. However, he never reached this goal. In fact, everything went terribly wrong. So why do we remember Shackleton? Because of the great leadership he showed during the trip. **E2** Shackleton left England in 1914 on the ship the *Endurance*. He had a crew of twenty-eight men, including the ship's officers and sailors, and some scientists who came along to do research. In January 1915, they entered the Antarctic Circle. However, it was colder than normal, and the ocean was full of ice, and the *Endurance* soon became stuck. Shackleton and his crew realized they'd have to wait ten months, until November—which is springtime in the Antarctic Circle—for the ice to melt. **E3** So, there they lived, on the ship, stuck in the ice, and waiting for spring. Now Shackleton—who was called "the boss" by his men—kept the morale up by keeping them busy. Now, in those days, ships' officers and scientists didn't usually interact with sailors. The officers and scientists usually got better food and lived in better conditions. But Shackleton needed everyone to work as a team and not as individuals. So everyone shared the jobs on the ship: The officers and scientists labored right beside the sailors cleaning the floors, and the sailors helped with the science experiments. Everyone ate the same food together at the same table. And

consequently, the men all became friends and learned to work together. **E4** Over the long winter, as the ship floated with the ice, the ice began to crush the ship. The crew could hear the awful sound of the wood bending and breaking as the ice closed in. And so in October of 1915, Shackleton ordered everyone to move off the ship and onto the ice. For nearly a month, they lived on the ice, next to the dying ship, watching it get slowly crushed. **E5** Then on November 21, 1915, with Shackleton's cry of "She's going, boys!" the men watched, horrified, as the *Endurance* came apart and sank into the water. **E6** But even when everything seemed hopeless, Shackleton didn't give up. He promised his men that if they worked hard and stayed together, they would get home. Now, at this point, Shackleton's leadership style was very important to the survival of the crew. Because of the way he treated the men—treating each man with respect—the crew became extremely loyal. They believed in him. If Shackleton believed they would get home, well, the men believed it, too. **E7** With the arrival of summer in March of 1916, the ice they had been living on began to melt. At this point, Shackleton and his men knew that they had to get to land. Now, they had floated close enough to see Elephant Island, a small, rocky island about 100 miles off in the distance. So in April, Shackleton and the crew got into three small boats they had saved from the ship. And after seven days of rough water and freezing temperatures, they finally made it to Elephant Island. It had been 467 days—more than a year since the men had stood on land. However, they still had absolutely no hope of rescue. No one knew where they were. **E8** At this point, Shackleton made his riskiest decision yet. He decided to take one of their small boats and sail back to a whaling station on South Georgia, an island about 800 miles away, and get help. He left Elephant Island with five men, promising to return and rescue the others. After seventeen days of sailing through some of the roughest waters in the world, Shackleton and the five men finally made it to South Georgia— amazingly. However, they still had to walk for thirty-six hours over ice-covered mountains to reach the whaling station. So the job wasn't done. And when they walked inside, as the story goes, the station manager took one look at these guys and said, "Who are you?" It had been so long that everyone thought Shackleton and his crew were dead. **E9** Over the next four months, Shackleton tried three times to rescue the men back on Elephant Island. But the sea was still full of ice, and the ships couldn't make it. Meanwhile, the men on Elephant Island were surviving, but had started to lose hope. They began to think that Shackleton had never made it to South Georgia, and that they'd be stuck in Antarctica forever. **E10** Then on August 30, 1916, nearly two years after their trip had begun, the men saw a ship approaching in the distance. They ran to the beach, waving and shouting. It was Shackleton, coming to rescue them! Shackleton, from the ship, counted the men on shore and cried with happiness when he saw that they'd all survived. He'd kept his promise to them. **E11** For this, Shackleton is credited as one of the great heroes of the time. Not for reaching his original goal, but for leading his men through some of the worst conditions in the world, and keeping his promise to them to bring them home alive.

Coaching Tips

[1] Note-taking: Using timelines When a speaker talks about historical events, a timeline can be a helpful way to record the events in your notes. As the speaker gives more information and dates, you can add on to your timeline. Your notes might look something like this: [see video for note-taking example]. A timeline can help you see the chronological order of events. It can also help you see the "big picture," or how individual events look all together. **[2] Critical Thinking: Using your imagination** The speaker says that everyone on the *Endurance* had to work as a team. What kinds of activities can you imagine people doing on a ship? Write down your ideas, and then listen to see if any of them match the activities the lecturer mentions. **[3] Note-taking: Reviewing** At this point in the story, how much time has passed since the men left England? Where have they been in that time? What's happened? Reviewing your notes briefly during a lecture can help you find mistakes and identify any missing information. **[4] Note-taking: Noting numbers** You've heard a lot of figures, or numbers, in this lecture. Are you writing out the number words or using digits? It's easier and faster to use digits. For example, you just heard "about eight hundred miles." How did you note that information? You may have written it like this: [see video for note-taking example]. Or maybe you've created your own abbreviations and symbols.

Talk about the Topic *page 98*

Hannah: . . . I didn't see it either.

River: Guys, I think we're supposed to be talking about the lecture we heard today.

Mia: Oh right, Shackleton!

Manny: Wow! That was a great story! That guy Shackleton, he was a great leader. There's no doubt that without great leadership, the ending would've been way different.

River: I was thinking the same thing. It's unbelievable how they survived all that cold weather, and not one person died.

Hannah: Yeah, so, I'm curious about everyone's thoughts: What was it about this guy that made him such a great leader?

Mia: Hmm, I'd say his treatment of everyone as equals. You know, like how he made the scientists clean the floors alongside the sailors.

River: Yeah, exactly—that would definitely give you a team feeling. Especially under such bad conditions.

Manny: Hmm, I agree somewhat. But I think it was the big decisions he made. I mean, how many times did he decide to move forward instead of just waiting for someone to help?

Hannah: True. First, off the ship and onto the ice, then from the ice to Elephant Island.

River: Then from Elephant Island to the whaling station. And then something like three tries before he finally rescued the other men?

Manny: Yeah. See? Like I said: great leadership! People need great leaders, or they just panic or give up.

Mia: Yeah.

Hannah: Yeah.

River: That is so true.

Hannah: I agree.

Manny: That's why I'm running for class president.

River: Really? I didn't know that. Congratulations!

Mia: Oh! Good luck with that!

Take the Unit Test

1. What is the main purpose of the lecture?
2. What topic is *not* discussed in the lecture?
3. What was the goal of Shackleton's trip to Antarctica?
4. How did Shackleton teach the crew to work as a team?
5. Why did Shackleton order the crew off the ship and onto the ice?
6. When did Shackleton say "She's going, boys!"
7. Why was the crew loyal to Shackleton?
8. Why did Shackleton and his crew go to Elephant Island?
9. Listen to this excerpt from the lecture: *After seventeen days of sailing through some of the roughest waters in the world, Shackleton and the five men finally made it to South Georgia— amazingly.* What is the speaker suggesting here?
10. Why is Shackleton remembered today? Choose *two* answers.

Extend the Topic *page 100*

Reporter: On April 11, 1970, the United States launched the *Apollo 13* mission with the goal of landing three astronauts on the moon. The year before, the U.S. had made two successful moon landings, so everyone thought that this trip would also go well. And for the first two days of the *Apollo 13* flight, it did. However, on the third day, there was an explosion in the spaceship and it started losing air. Thus began one of the most amazing stories in the history of space exploration. The crew soon found out that the spaceship was damaged. They had problems with their power and electricity. And later, they started to run out of water. They worried that the computers on the ship would stop working. All of these problems had to be solved quickly by the crew, working as a team with the people on the ground. Six days after their flight began, on April 17, all three crewmen returned safely to Earth, landing successfully in the ocean.

ANSWER KEY

Build Your Vocabulary *pages 93–94*
A. 1. a 2. b 3. b 4. a 5. a 6. a 7. b 8. b 9. a 10. b 11. b 12. a 13. b 14. a **B. Interact with Vocabulary!** 1. d 2. f 3. g 4. a 5. c 6. b 7. e 8. j 9. h 10. m 11. k 12. i 13. n 14. l

Focus Your Attention *page 95*
A. <u>8/1/1914</u> London → Buenos Aries, Argentina; <u>4 mos.</u> → Antarctic Circle; <u>10/26</u> Argentina → whaling station, South Georgia; <u>12/5</u> South Georgia → Antarctica

Listen for Main Ideas *pages 96–97*
B 1. 1914 2. Jan. 1915 3. 10 months 4. Oct. 1915 5. Nov. 21, 1915 6. Mar. 1916 7. April 1916 8. 17 9. 36 10. Aug. 30, 1916

Listen for Details *page 97*
B. *Suggested corrections:* 1. F (Shackleton's goal was to walk across Antarctica.) 2. T 3. F (Shackleton had crew members work together to become friends and work as a team.) 4. F (In October 1915, the crew moved onto the ice because the ice was crushing the ship.) 5. T 6. F (Shackleton and five men traveled 800 miles by boat to South Georgia.) 7. T 8. F (Shackleton rescued his crew on Elephant Island after trying three times.)

Talk about the Topic *page 98*
A. *Suggested answers:* 1. Mia, Manny, River 2. Manny, Hannah, River **B.** Asking for opinions or ideas: 3; Expressing an opinion: 2, 4; Keeping the discussion on topic: 1

Review Your Notes *page 99*
Suggested answers:

Endurance Timeline
- **1914:** Shackleton's goal is to lead group across Antarctica on foot
- Ship leaves England
- **1915:** Ship enters the Antarctic Circle
- Ship becomes stuck in ice; must wait 10 months for spring
- Shackleton keeps morale up; keeps men busy
- Oct. 1915: Ice crushes ship
- Nov. 21, 1915: Ship sinks
- **1916:** Summer arrives
- Mar. 1916: Ice begins to melt
- Shackleton and crew sail in 3 boats to Elephant Island
- Shackleton and 5 men sail to South Georgia; Shackleton and men walk for 36 hours
- Shackleton returns to Elephant Island to rescue others

Take the Unit Test
1. a 2. d 3. d 4. b 5. a 6. b 7. c 8. c 9. d 10. a and d

Extend the Topic *page 100*
B. 1. b 2. a 3. b 4. b

UNIT 10 TEST   HISTORY: Shackleton

Listen to each question. Circle the letter of the correct answer.

1. a. to tell the story of Sir Ernest Shackleton and the *Endurance*
   b. to compare two Antarctic explorers
   c. to give advice about how to be a good leader
   d. to point out the mistakes Shackleton made

2. a. Shackleton's leadership style
   b. the problems Shackleton had during the trip
   c. Shackleton's goal
   d. what happened after Shackleton returned home

3. a. to be the first to live in Antarctica for a long time
   b. to be the first to reach Antarctica
   c. to be the first to sail around Antarctica
   d. to be the first to walk across Antarctica

4. a. by giving some people better food than others
   b. by making everyone live and work together as equals
   c. by making sure the sailors respected the ship's officers
   d. by making the crew work quickly

5. a. because the ice was crushing the ship
   b. because they could find more food on the ice
   c. because they had more room on the ice
   d. because the ship sank into the water

6. a. when the *Endurance* got stuck in the ice
   b. when the *Endurance* sank
   c. when the crew left for Elephant Island
   d. when he rescued the crew

7. a. because he knew a lot about Antarctica
   b. because he made risky decisions
   c. because he treated each man with respect
   d. because he was the leader of the trip

8. a. because there was a whaling station there
   b. because they had to move off the ship
   c. because the ice they lived on was melting
   d. because they thought some other people might be there

9. a. that Shackleton made the wrong decision to go to South Georgia
   b. that Shackleton thought the trip would be easier
   c. that Shackleton was surprised when he reached South Georgia
   d. that the trip to South Georgia was very dangerous

10. a. because of his leadership of the crew
    b. because he treated his crew badly
    c. because he made many bad decisions
    d. because he brought all of his men home alive

UNIT 11 PHILOSOPHY
Ethics

TEACHING TIPS

UNIT OVERVIEW

In this unit, students will discuss different approaches to making ethical decisions. The lecture covers two approaches: the rights approach and the utilitarian approach. In follow-up projects, students discuss situations requiring ethical decisions.

Connect to the Topic *page 102*   *~10 minutes*

As a warm-up activity, consider having students study the photo of the girl with the found billfold and guess what the unit will be about. In the introduction, students learn the definitions of the terms *ethics* and *philosopher*. Then they work in groups to discuss their choices in different ethical situations.

Build Your Vocabulary *pages 103–104*   *~15 minutes*

Students study the following words and phrases related to philosophy and ethics:

actions	greatest good	overall
allows	have an issue with	principle
banned	in principle	put a ban on
be allowed to	individual	right
community	majority	the right to
the effects of	majority of	tax
freedom	make choices about	unethical
the freedom to	make decisions	utilitarian

For the Interact with Vocabulary! activity, you may want to encourage students to first notice the boldfaced words. Figuring out these collocations can help students more quickly unscramble the sentences.

Focus Your Attention *page 105*   *~10 minutes*

Students learn cues that lecturers use to introduce examples:

For instance . . .	*Let's look at an example . . .*
For example . . .	*Let's say that . . .*
Let's take _____ as an example . . .	*Through this example, we can see . . .*

Listen to the Lecture *pages 106–107*   *~30 minutes*

Students consider the definitions of *rights* and *utilitarian* (Before You Listen) before listening to the unit lecture on approaches to ethical decisions. They use their notes to answer multiple-choice questions (Listen for Main Ideas) and check statements that correctly describe each approach (Listen for Details).
Lecture video time: 6 min. 27 sec.   *Number of episodes: 10*

Talk about the Topic *page 108*   *~20 minutes*

Four students—Michael, May, Yhinny, and Qiang—discuss the lecture. Part A focuses on matching these students with ideas from the discussion. In Part B, your students work on these discussion strategies:

- Expressing an opinion: "Personally, I believe I should have the right to talk on the phone while I'm in my car."
- Offering a fact or example: "Drivers using cell phones have something like four times more accidents."
- Keeping the discussion on topic: "OK. Anyway, what about the utilitarian side?"

BONUS ACTIVITY

You can supplement this activity by having students compare their opinions with the opinions of the students in the discussion.

For Part C, students are encouraged to use the discussion strategies they've learned. They may use phrases from the student discussion or they may come up with their own.
Student discussion video time: 1 min. 23 sec.

Review Your Notes *page 109*   *~15 minutes*

Students focus on reconstructing their notes, paying attention to details about each of the approaches to ethical decision making discussed in the lecture.

BONUS ACTIVITY

You can supplement this activity by having students use their notes to summarize parts of the lecture with a partner.

Take the Unit Test *Teacher's Pack page 67*   *~15 minutes*

You may want to play the lecture again just before giving the test. Students answer standard test questions about the content of the lecture. Specifically, the test covers the following: the development of the rights and utilitarian approaches, the most important aspects of these approaches, and the examples discussed in the lecture.

Extend the Topic *pages 110–111*   *~30 minutes*

- Listening and Discussion: Students listen to and discuss a call to a radio show on ethics.
- Project/Presentation: Students create and discuss different situations that require ethical decisions.

Focus Your Attention:
Try It Out! *page 105*

Speaker: Every day, we have to make many ethical decisions—many decisions about right and wrong. Let's look at a real-world example: Maybe this has happened to you? Let's say that you are buying something in the store. And the clerk at the store makes a mistake and gives you too much change. What do you do? You have an ethical decision: Do you keep the money? Or do you tell the clerk about the mistake and give the money back? Interesting situation, hm? Well, through this example, we can see that ethics is something we can use in our everyday lives . . .

Listen for Main Ideas and Listen
for Details *pages 106–107*

Philosophy lecturer: E1 Every day, we have to make decisions—we have to ask ourselves, What's the right thing to do and what's the wrong thing to do? But how do we make these decisions? How do we know what's right and wrong? The study of ethics can give us some answers. Today I'd like to talk about two different approaches, two different ways to make ethical decisions: the rights approach and the utilitarian approach. So, first I'll explain each approach, and then we'll see how these work in real-world examples. E2 First let's talk about the rights approach. We use the idea of rights to talk about many ethical problems. This idea of rights comes originally from the philosophy of Immanuel Kant, a German philosopher in the eighteenth century. The principle says that each individual has the freedom to make choices, and that other people must respect those choices. E3 Let's take the right to free speech as an example. Freedom of speech means two things: first, that I have the right to say whatever I want, and second, that other people must respect my right to speak. So according to the rights approach, an ethical action must respect an individual's choices—the power of the individual to make his or her own decisions. To decide if an action is ethical using the rights approach, we must always ask: How does this action affect the individual's freedom to make choices? E4 Now, let's look at another approach—the utilitarian approach. That's u-t-i-l-i-t-a-r-i-a-n. The utilitarian approach was made popular in the nineteenth century by British philosopher John Stuart Mill. In this approach, the most important thing is not individual rights. The most important thing is making the world a better place. So here an ethical action is one that creates the greatest amount of good. E5 Let's take, for example, paying taxes. The government collects taxes from individual people. Now, most people don't like paying taxes because they have less money to spend on other things. However, taxes help the community as a whole, paying for things like hospitals, roads, schools, parks—things that benefit everyone. So, even though paying taxes is bad for some people individually, it's good for the majority—for most people in the community. So to decide if an action is ethical following the utilitarian approach, we must ask: What action will cause the greatest good for the most people? E6 Now, let's take a real-world example and look at how to make a decision using these two approaches—that is, the rights approach and the utilitarian approach. Let's look at the question of public smoking. Starting in the late 1990s, this became an issue in many places when smoking was banned in office buildings, schools, restaurants, and so on. The question is, how do we make a decision about whether to ban smoking or not? E7 When you look at the problem from the rights approach, we have to ask: How does smoking in public affect individual rights? And we have to look at the rights of two groups of people: smokers and nonsmokers. So, first let's look at the rights of smokers. Smokers will say that they should be free to smoke wherever they want, and that other people should respect that right, even if they don't like it. But, what about nonsmokers? Nonsmokers say that they should be free to breathe clean air, and that smokers should respect that right. Smokers shouldn't force people to breathe their cigarette smoke. This, however, shows us one of the problems of using the rights approach because when you have two groups, how do you decide whose rights are more important: smokers' or nonsmokers'? E8 For another point of view, let's take the utilitarian approach. Following that approach, we have to ask: What creates the greatest amount of good? Allowing smoking in public places? Or banning it? So, what's good about allowing smoking in public places? Well, smokers will be happy. But, that's pretty much it. But it causes a lot of harm. E9 So overall, you can argue that the ethical choice is to impose a ban on smoking in public places because it creates the greater good: Public places will be healthier, and we'll save money on health costs because fewer people will get sick. Through this example, we can see the differences between looking at an ethical problem from the rights approach and from the utilitarian approach. E10 So, until next time, I'd like you to think of some other real-life examples and consider them in the context of the two ethical decision-making approaches we discussed today. That's all.

Coaching Tips

[1] **Note-taking: Using charts** The speaker gives the names of two approaches. He says he'll explain each and then give examples from the real world. How can you set up your notes for the information that's to come? Here's one idea: [see video for note-taking example]. [2] **Note-taking: Using abbreviations** The speaker says, "Let's take the right to free speech as an example." A fast way to identify something in your notes as an example is to use the abbreviation *e.g.* or *ex.* Since there are several examples in this lecture, try abbreviating the word *example* as you take notes. Having examples clearly identified in your notes can help you find them easily when you go to review. [3] **Critical Thinking: Responding to a topic** Do you agree with the speaker's conclusion that a smoking ban is the ethical choice? Are there ways of looking at the issue of smoking in public places that the speaker didn't consider? How do you feel about smoking in public? [4] **Critical thinking: Thinking of examples** The speaker tells you to think about other real-life examples using the two ethical decision-making approaches he has explained. When you review your notes, try adding your own examples. Coming up with your own examples will make reviewing your notes more interesting and help you better understand a new concept.

Talk about the Topic *page 108*

Yhinny: You know, I'm still a little unclear on how the rights approach compares to the utilitarian approach.

May: Well, we're supposed to create our own example, so maybe that'll help?

Michael: OK, well, I've got an example: if we think about using cell phones while driving. So, from a rights approach, we would look at the rights of the person driving, yeah?

May: Uh-huh.

Qiang: Well, personally, I believe I should have the right to talk on the phone while I'm in my car. Because it's my car and my phone.

May: So, you're saying, you're like the smoker having the right to smoke wherever.

Qiang: Yeah, but there's a huge difference. I mean, talking on the phone doesn't really hurt anyone's health.

May: Oh!

Michael: Oh, I disagree!

Yhinny: I don't think so.

Michael: Drivers using cell phones have something like four times more accidents.

Qiang: Where'd you hear that?

Michael: I don't know, some government study or something.

Yhinny: OK. Anyway, what about the, the utilitarian side?

May: OK, well, lots of drivers pay more attention to their phone conversations than the road, which is dangerous, right?

Michael: Right. So society in general suffers.

May: Exactly.

Qiang: OK, OK! Cell phone use should be prohibited while driving.

[Phone rings.]

Yhinny: And in study groups!

Qiang: Sorry!

Take the Unit Test

1. What is the main purpose of the lecture?
2. Where did the idea of the rights approach come from?
3. Which of these describes an ethical decision based on the rights approach?
4. When did the utilitarian approach become popular?
5. What is most important under the utilitarian approach?
6. Why does the speaker mention paying taxes?
7. In the example of public smoking, which rights does the speaker discuss? Choose *two* answers.
8. What is the problem with using the rights approach to decide about public smoking?
9. Following the utilitarian approach, why is banning smoking the ethical decision?
10. Listen to this excerpt from the lecture. *So, what's good about allowing smoking in public places? Well, smokers will be happy. But, that's pretty much it. But it causes a lot of harm.* What is the speaker suggesting here?

Extend the Topic *page 110*

Dr. Ethics: This is Dr. Ethics, and I'm here to answer your ethics questions. Hi, caller. What do you got for me?

Caller: Hi, this is Michelle. I love your show.

Dr. Ethics: Thank you, thank you. Your question?

Caller: Oh, well, my husband and I have a disagreement. You see, he has a computer at home that he uses. He uses it mostly to play games and surf the Internet, stuff like that. But now that our kids are in school, they'd like to use the computer sometimes. They have to do research on the Internet and write papers. And frankly, I'd like to be able to check my e-mail once in a while. But my husband says no, he paid for it, it's his computer, and he should be able to use it whenever he wants. My feeling is, we're a family, and whatever we own belongs to everybody. What do you think?

Dr. Ethics: Hmm. This seems like a case of individual rights versus the common good, no? I mean, your husband feels that, since he bought the computer, he has a right to use it and not share it. On the other hand, you have the needs of you and your kids. And the kids need the computer to do their homework, right? And your "need"—that one is in air quotes, but I'll give it to you—to check your

e-mail. So although we fellas like to stick together, I have to agree with you, Michelle, even though your husband has a right to his computer, the greater good of the family is more important.

Caller: Woo-hoo! Thank you, Dr. Ethics. Very helpful . . .

ANSWER KEY

Build Your Vocabulary *pages 103–104*

A. 1. c 2. b 3. a 4. c 5. a 6. b 7. a 8. b 9. c 10. b 11. a 12. c **B. Interact with Vocabulary!** 1. the freedom to make choices 2. must make choices about 3. the effects of our actions on 4. help us make good decisions 5. the greater good in principle only 6. to put a ban on free speech 7. the right to free speech 8. majority of people in my community 9. have an issue with 10. should be allowed to enjoy

Focus Your Attention *page 105*

A. <u>ethical</u> decisions; Clerk—<u>makes a mistake</u>; Do you: <u>keep</u> $ OR <u>give</u> $ back?

Listen for Main Ideas *pages 106–107*

B. 1. c 2. b 3. c 4. b

Listen for Details *page 107*

B. Individual rights: 1, 3, 6, 7, 9; Utilitarianism: 2, 4, 5, 8, 10, 11

Talk about the Topic *page 108*

A. 1. Qiang 2. Michael, May, Yhinny, Qiang
B. Expressing an opinion: 1, 2; Offering a fact or example: 3; Keeping the discussion on topic: 4

Review Your Notes *page 109*

	Rights	Utilitarian
1st per. to describe this approach:	Immanuel Kant, 18th c. German philosopher	John Stuart Mill, 19th c. British philosopher
Ex. of this approach:	free speech	paying taxes
Most important thing about this approach:	ind'l. rights	making the world a better place/good for majority
How this approach sees/addresses public smoking:	smokers can smoke anywhere	no smoking in public places b/c of greater good

Take the Unit Test

1. a 2. b 3. b 4. c 5. c 6. b 7. b and c 8. a 9. a 10. b

Extend the Topic *page 110*

A. 1. The husband feels that since he paid for the computer, only he has a right to use it. The wife feels that he should share it with the family.
2. Dr. Ethics thinks that the husband should share the computer. It will serve the greater good of the family because the children can do homework and the wife can check her e-mail.

PHILOSOPHY: Ethics

 Listen to each question. Circle the letter of the correct answer.

1. a. to compare two ethical approaches
    b. to convince students to make ethical decisions
    c. to explain which ethical approach is best
    d. to tell the history of how ethical approaches have changed

2. a. the idea of freedom of speech
    b. the philosophy of Immanuel Kant
    c. the study of ethics
    d. the writing of John Stuart Mill

3. a. a decision that allows people to do whatever they want
    b. a decision that gives individuals the freedom to make choices
    c. a decision that is best for most people
    d. a decision that makes everyone happy

4. a. in the seventeenth century
    b. in the eighteenth century
    c. in the nineteenth century
    d. in the twentieth century

5. a. being fair and treating everyone equally
    b. making sure that people are free to choose
    c. making the world a better place
    d. stopping people from being hurt

6. a. to explain how governments raise money for roads and schools
    b. to give an example of the utilitarian approach
    c. to point out that no one likes to pay taxes
    d. to show the problems of using the rights approach

7. a. the right of governments to ban the selling of cigarettes
    b. the right of nonsmokers to breathe fresh air
    c. the right of smokers to smoke wherever they want
    d. the right of employers to ban smoking

8. a. It can be difficult to decide whose rights are most important.
    b. Most people don't understand the idea of rights.
    c. Smokers don't have any rights.
    d. Nonsmokers' rights are more important.

9. a. because it will create the greatest amount of good for the community
    b. because it will make everyone happy
    c. because it will make nonsmokers happy
    d. because it will respect the rights of smokers

10. a. It's good to allow smoking in public.
    b. Smoking in public is good only for smokers.
    c. Smoking will make people happy.
    d. It makes everyone happy when people can smoke in public.

UNIT 12 ECONOMICS
Opportunity Cost

UNIT OVERVIEW

In this unit, students will learn about the concept of opportunity cost and how it can be used to make economic choices as well as choices in everyday life. The lecture explains the concept of opportunity cost and shows how it can be used to make decisions. In follow-up projects, students role-play different situations that require making choices.

Connect to the Topic *page 112*   *~10 minutes*

As a warm-up activity, considering having students discuss the kinds of choices the people in each photo have (for example, buying a new car instead of saving for retirement; going to a farmer's market instead of sleeping in; going into business with a partner instead of working alone, etc.). In the introduction, students learn the meaning of *economics*. Then they rank several activities based on how they would choose to spend their time. They discuss their answers in groups.

Build Your Vocabulary *pages 113–114*   *~15 minutes*

Students study the following words and phrases related to economics and the concept of opportunity cost:

breaks down	focus	option of
come out with	fund	options
compete	give up	outcome
compete with	invest	put funds toward
concepts	invest in	put money into
elements	opportunities	valuable
excludes	opportunity to	widgets

For the Interact with Vocabulary! activity, you may want to encourage students to first notice the boldfaced words and explain that they form collocations when paired with the correct word.

Focus Your Attention *page 115*   *~10 minutes*

Students learn words and phrases that lecturers use to show causes and effects:

Signaling causes:	**Signaling effects:**
If . . .	*. . . then . . .*
. . . because . . .	*. . . causes . . .*
Since . . .	*. . . so . . .*

Listen to the Lecture *pages 116–117*   *~30 minutes*

Students consider the definition of *opportunity cost* (Before You Listen) before listening to the unit lecture about the concept of opportunity cost. They use their notes to answer true/false questions (Listen for Main Ideas) and complete a set of incomplete notes (Listen for Details).
Lecture video time: 5 min. 49 sec.   *Number of episodes: 9*

Talk about the Topic *page 118*   *~20 minutes*

Four students—Ayman, Molly, Rob, and Alana—discuss the lecture. Part A focuses on matching these students with ideas from the discussion. In Part B, your students work on these discussion strategies:

- Agreeing: "Yeah, I agree."
- Disagreeing: "Really? . . . For me, the widget example worked better . . ."
- Keeping the discussion on topic: "Anyway—back to the widget example . . ."

BONUS ACTIVITY

You can supplement this activity by having students compare their opinions with the opinions of the students in the discussion.

For Part C, students are encouraged to use the discussion strategies they've learned. They may use phrases from the student discussion or they may come up with their own.
Student discussion video time: 1 min. 33 sec.

Review Your Notes *page 119*   *~15 minutes*

Students focus on reconstructing their notes, paying attention to the examples discussed in the lecture and the results of different decisions in those examples.

BONUS ACTIVITY

You can supplement this activity by having students use their notes to summarize parts of the lecture with a partner.

Take the Unit Test *Teacher's Pack page 73*   *~15 minutes*

You may want to play the lecture again just before giving the test. Students answer standard test questions about the content of the lecture. Spceifically, the test covers the following: the definition of opportunity cost and why it is useful, and how the concept of opportunity cost applies to the examples in the lecture.

Extend the Topic *pages 120–121*   *~30 minutes*

- Listening and Discussion: Students listen to and discuss a blogcaster's description of a choice about buying a morning cup of coffee.
- Project/Presentation: Students work in groups to create and perform role plays about situations in which people must consider the opportunity cost of their decisions.

Focus Your Attention:
Try It Out! *page 115*

Speaker: Now, I want to look at advertising—we all know that advertising is a good way for a company to increase its sales. But how much should a company spend? And which kind of advertising should they choose? Advertising is expensive, so companies need to consider their options carefully. For example, if a company chooses to run a TV commercial, then more people may learn about their product. On the other hand, if they run a newspaper ad, then they'll save money. But they may reach fewer people. Because advertising decisions can be complicated, companies should start by doing some marketing research. So you see, with every decision . . .

Listen for Main Ideas and Listen for Details *pages 116–117*

Economics lecturer: **E1** Today we're going to talk about choices. Every day, in business and in our personal lives, we make choices. For instance, should I invest my money or spend it? Or what should I do with my time? We're going to look at a concept called opportunity cost. This concept is used all the time in economics and business—and in everyday life—because it's a good way to think about making choices and the "costs" involved. **E2** First, let's look at an example from everyday life. Say you have two hours of free time today. There are many ways you could spend your time, but only two that you're really interested in: cleaning your apartment or taking a nap. There's not time for both, so you have to choose. If you clean your apartment, you won't have time to take a nap. If you take a nap, you won't have time to clean your apartment. You must choose. And remember: Doing one thing means choosing not to do the other. **E3** This is what we call opportunity cost. Opportunity cost is the thing you give up to get something you want. Again: Opportunity cost is the thing you give up to get something you want. If you clean your apartment, the opportunity cost is taking a nap and feeling rested—you see that? On the other hand, if you take a nap, the opportunity cost is cleaning your apartment and having a clean living space. **E4** So this is the first important point about opportunity cost: The focus is not on what you get when you make a choice, but what you give up. Hence, by doing one thing, you lose the opportunity to do something else. That's what we mean by "cost." Another important point is that opportunity cost is

not about price or money. Instead, it's a way of looking at choices that don't have a price tag, like feeling rested after a nap. So this concept helps you to see the "cost" of your decisions. **E5** Now let's look at a business decision that has an opportunity cost. Let's say we have a company, International Widgets. I'm just using the term *widgets* to mean any product. It could mean cars, lipstick, frozen pizza. Whatever! The product we use here in the example isn't important. Anyway, International Widgets has been doing well, so we have extra money to invest in the company. We have two investment possibilities: One is to put the extra money into advertising—radio, newspaper ads, so on—so that more people will hear about the fantastic widgets we make and will buy more of them. The other possibility is to build a new factory so we can make more widgets. So we have to choose. If we choose to build a new factory, then the opportunity cost will be advertising and people hearing about our fantastic product. On the other hand, if we advertise, the opportunity cost will be a new factory to make more widgets. We might spend the same amount of money in each case, but the opportunity cost is different with each choice. **E6** Of course, many decisions are more complicated—have more "moving parts"—than that example. So let's add a third element. But first we need to look at our definition of opportunity cost again. Listen closely—this is important. Opportunity cost is the single, most valuable thing we give up to get what we want. It's not all of the choices that you give up. Opportunity cost is, by definition, the most valuable thing you give up. **E7** So, let's imagine that same situation with three elements: advertising, our factory, and our workers. Our widgets are selling like crazy. So, we don't need to advertise—right?—because the product is already really popular. However, we do need a new factory so we can make more widgets and have more widgets to sell. But the factory workers are also unhappy. They're working long hours, and they want to be paid more. And we're afraid they'll quit if we don't give them raises. In this case, if we decide to fund a new factory, the opportunity cost will be giving workers raises. That's the first thing we would do if we didn't put our funds into a new factory. It's the most valuable thing we give up. It's our opportunity cost. **E8** Now let's look at the same three choices, but with a different outcome. Let's say the workers are well paid and happy for now, so we can exclude the option of giving them a raise. It's not necessary. But our factory's old, starting to break down, so we need a new factory. In addition, another company has come out with a very similar product, and they're advertising a lot. So we also want to advertise more to compete and to keep our sales numbers high. In this case, if we fund a new factory, the opportunity cost will be advertising—it's what we would do if we didn't choose to build a new factory. E9 Well, I hope these examples help explain the concept of opportunity cost, and you can see how useful this way of thinking is when making decisions. Next time, we'll look at more examples of how we can use the idea of opportunity cost.

Coaching Tips

[1] **Listening: Identifying cause and effect** In this lecture, you're hearing about cause and effect. The speaker explains that if you do A, then the effect is that you can't do B. Words signaling cause include *if, because,* and *since.* Words signaling effect include *then, so,* and *will cause.* Try to listen for these words to help you identify the causes and effects in the examples the lecturer is presenting.

[2] **Listening: Recognizing irrelevant details** Not every word of a lecture is important. Speakers will often signal when information they have just given isn't necessary to note down. Here, the speaker lists several items and then says, "Whatever!" With this, the speaker tells you that her list of items was not an important detail. Knowing what *not* to note will help you keep your notes organized and clear.

[3] **Listening: Listening for definitions** The speaker gives a more detailed definition of *opportunity cost.* How is this definition different from the earlier definition? When a speaker adds to a definition or information that was given earlier, you can expect the lecture to continue in the direction of this new information. [4] **Note-taking: Summarizing** The speaker has just given a fourth example of opportunity cost. Can you think of a way to summarize all of the examples you've heard? Here's an idea: [see video for note-taking example]. Rewriting or summarizing your notes is a great way to make sure you understand and know the information.

Talk about the Topic *page 118*

Ayman: So what did you guys think about the lecture?

Molly: I thought it was really interesting. I mean, she had a lot of points that I've never heard before that I thought were just really practical and really accessible.

Rob: Yeah, I agree.

Ayman: Hey guys, I have a question.

Alana: Uh-huh.

Ayman: So, in my notes, I wrote this "opportunity cost" concept in my own words. Can I get your opinions?

Rob: Yeah.

Ayman: So, I wrote: "Opportunity cost is the 'price tag' on the opportunity."

Alana: Uh-huh.

Ayman: . . . this means the value of the thing I *didn't* choose.

Rob: That's actually a really good way to express it.

Molly: Yeah that's really good. This concept seems so useful to me. You know, in the future, I'm going to consider the "cost" of my choices before I make a decision. You know?

Rob: Do you remember the example that she used about taking a nap versus cleaning your apartment?

Molly: Yeah, that was a great example.

Rob: That was the one that made it really clear to me.

Alana: Really?

Rob: I liked it.

Alana: Really?

Rob: Yeah.

Alana: Hmm. For me, the widget example worked better.

Ayman: But what is a widget?

Rob: Well, she just means, like, any object or thing. There really is no such thing as a widget but just as an example.

Ayman: Oh. OK.

Alana: Anyway—back to the widget example. We're always making decisions—and not just two or three, but many choices at one time.

Molly: Yeah, you know, frankly, I'm not that interested in business and economics and stuff.

Rob: No!

Molly: Yeah, but this really made it all kind of practical. You know?

Ayman: Yeah, it is kind of interesting.

Alana: Yeah.

Rob: It was! It kept me awake.

Take the Unit Test

1. What is the main purpose of the lecture?
2. Why does the speaker give the example of cleaning your apartment versus taking a nap?
3. What is opportunity cost?
4. How is the idea of opportunity cost useful?
5. Why does the speaker use the term *widgets*?
6. Listen to this excerpt from the lecture: *Of course, many decisions are more complicated—have more "moving parts"—than that example. So let's add a third element.* What is the speaker suggesting here?
7. When there are three or more choices, what is the opportunity cost?
8. If we need a new factory and our workers want raises, what is the opportunity cost of building a new factory?

9. In the example of International Widgets, the speaker mentions all of the following choices *except* which one?
10. Which of these statements would the speaker agree with?

Extend the Topic *page 120*

Blogcaster: Every morning, I go down to a local cafe and get a cup of coffee before work, a nice cup of coffee to start the day. But the other day, I started thinking about the opportunity cost of that cup of coffee. What am I giving up by getting it every day? Well, first, there's the time. It takes me maybe fifteen minutes. Not much time. But if I didn't get that coffee, I could get to the office fifteen minutes earlier. Then there's the money I spend on it. Again, not much. But I could spend that money on something else. But then I thought, I do this every day. The cost really adds up! In one week, I spend about $10 and more than an hour waiting in line to get coffee! In one hour, I can get a lot of work done. And I'd rather save the $10 for something important, like the new car I want to buy. So anyway, I decided to make a change. I decided that the opportunity cost was too much. So now, I have a quick cup at home as I get ready. I don't go to the café any more. I wonder if they miss me?

ANSWER KEY

Build Your Vocabulary *pages 113–114*

A. 1. b 2. c 3. a 4. c 5. a 6. b 7. b 8. c 9. a 10. d 11. a 12. c 13. b **B. Interact with Vocabulary!** 1. up 2. in 3. down 4. to 5. of 6. toward 7. out 8. with 9. into

Focus Your Attention *page 115*

A. <u>cause (reason)</u>: run newspaper ad; because advertising decisions complicated; <u>effect (result)</u>: more people learn about product

Listen for Main Ideas *page 116*

B. 1. T 2. F (useful for making many kinds of decisions) 3. F (not the amount of money you pay for something, but the most valuable thing you give up) 4. T 5. F (two or more choices)

Listen for Details *page 117*

B. Ex 1: <u>2</u> hrs of free time; Choices: <u>Clean apt.</u> / <u>take nap</u>; <u>Take nap</u> / <u>clean apt.</u>; Opp. cost of cleaning apt. = <u>taking nap</u>; Opp. cost of taking nap = <u>cleaning apt.</u> Ex 2: extra <u>$$ (money)</u>; Choices: <u>advertising</u> OR build <u>new factory</u>; Opp. cost = <u>new factory</u>; Opp. cost = <u>advertising</u>; Ex 3: don't need to <u>advertise</u>; Need new <u>factory</u>; Workers want <u>raises</u>; Fund <u>new factory</u> opp. cost = <u>raises for workers</u>; Ex. 4: Workers <u>happy</u>; Factory starting to <u>get old, starting to break down</u>; Other co. has <u>similar product</u>—need to <u>advertise</u>; opp. cost = <u>advertising</u>

Talk about the Topic *page 118*

A. *Suggested answers:* 1. Molly, Rob 2. Rob 3. Alana **B.** Agreeing: 1, 2; Disagreeing: 3; Keeping the discussion on topic: 4

Review Your Notes *page 119*

def: the most valuable thing you give up to get something you want; is *not* all of the things you give up

Ex. 1	clean apartment/take nap	cleaning apartment is taking a nap (+ reverse)
Ex. 2	advertise/build factory	building factory is advertising (+ reverse)
Ex. 3: • <u>popular</u> • <u>new factory</u> • <u>unhappy</u>	build new factory/give raises	building factory is giving raises (+ reverse)
Ex. 4: • <u>happy</u> • <u>factory</u> • <u>advertising</u>	fund factory/buy ads	funding new factory is advertising (+ reverse)

Take the Unit Test

1. d 2. a 3. b 4. a 5. b 6. b 7. a 8. c 9. c 10. d

Extend the Topic *page 120*

B. 1. To buy a cup of coffee every morning or not 2. $10 and an hour of time 3. Getting more work done and saving money for a new car 4. She decided to make coffee at home and drink it as she gets ready.

ECONOMICS: Opportunity Cost

UNIT 12 TEST

Listen to each question. Circle the letter of the correct answer.

1. a. to give several examples of business decisions
   b. to convince students to make good choices
   c. to compare different ways of making economic decisions
   d. to explain the concept of opportunity cost

2. a. to illustrate the idea of opportunity cost
   b. to describe common choices that students make
   c. to help the students make decisions in everyday life
   d. to convince the students to use their time better

3. a. the amount of money you pay to do something
   b. the thing you give up to get something else
   c. the number of choices you can make
   d. the best choice in any situation

4. a. It's a way of looking at choices that don't have a price tag.
   b. It can help you decide which choice will cost the most.
   c. It can be used in many different businesses.
   d. It is simple to use.

5. a. because the students are familiar with widgets
   b. because it is not important what product is used in the example
   c. because she wants to discuss many products
   d. because widgets are useful in business

6. a. Most decisions are too complicated to understand.
   b. Many decisions involve more than two choices.
   c. It's necessary to consider three elements before making a decision.
   d. Decisions often need to be changed.

7. a. the most valuable thing you give up
   b. all of the things you give up
   c. the thing you most want to do
   d. all of the possible things you can do

8. a. doing more advertising
   b. making a new product
   c. giving raises to the workers
   d. selling more widgets

9. a. advertising more
   b. building a new factory
   c. making a new product
   d. giving raises to the workers

10. a. Opportunity cost can only be used to make business decisions.
    b. Opportunity cost is difficult to understand.
    c. Opportunity cost works best for complicated decisions.
    d. Opportunity cost works for decisions in business and everyday life.